CAPE COD BAY

CAPE COD BAY
A HISTORY OF SALT & SEA

THERESA MITCHELL BARBO

FOREWORD *by* RICHARD G. GURNON
REAR ADMIRAL, USMS
President, MASSACHUSETTS MARITIME ACADEMY

Charleston · London
THE
History
PRESS

Published by The History Press
Charleston, SC 29403
www.historypress.net

Cover image: *Searsville*, a vessel constructed at the Shiverick Shipyards in East Dennis. *Artist unknown, courtesy of the Dennis Historical Society.*

Cover design by Natasha Momberger

First published 2008

Manufactured in the United States

ISBN 978.1.59629.502.5

Library of Congress Cataloging-in-Publication Data

Barbo, Theresa M.
Cape Cod Bay : a history of salt and sea / Theresa Mitchell Barbo.
p. cm.
Includes bibliographical references and index.
ISBN 978-1-59629-502-5
1. Cape Cod Bay (Mass.)--History. 2. Natural history--Massachusetts--Cape Cod Bay. 3. Cape Cod Bay (Mass.)--Environmental conditions. 4. Human ecology--Massachusetts--Cape Cod Bay. I. Title.
F72.C3B215 2008
551.46'1345--dc22
                              2008029857

Notice: The information in this book is true and complete to the best of our knowledge. It is offered without guarantee on the part of the author or The History Press. The author and The History Press disclaim all liability in connection with the use of this book.

For Dan

CONTENTS

FOREWORD

The sea surrounds us. Living on Cape Cod, it is both a physical fact and a way of life. When the Cape Cod Canal was opened in 1914—the same year as the more famous Panama Canal—it changed this sandy accumulation of glacially deposited debris from a peninsula that stuck out into the North Atlantic into an island stitched to the Massachusetts mainland by three fragile steel bridges. As Italy can be compared to the shape of a boot, Cape Cod looks from the air like the crooked arm of a bodybuilder, striking a pose that displays his biceps. The curved fist of Provincetown is at one end and the shoulder seam of the Cape Cod Canal is at the other. Contained within the protection of this arm is the treasure of Cape Cod Bay.

The early inhabitants of this narrow land were dependent on the bay for their very survival, but the cool Atlantic waters trapped by the crooked arm provided natural air conditioning and pleasant surroundings that offered relief from the hot summers of inland regions. When Europeans stumbled into Cape Cod Bay, they qualified as the first tourists—wide-eyed and weary, somewhat lost and irritating to the natives with their customs, accents and attitudes. Like their predecessors, they found the bay alive with marine animals and, as one Englishman was rumored to have said, "Codfish so thick one can walk on their backs." The settlers rejoiced at their wondrous discovery.

Founded in 1891 in Boston, the Massachusetts Maritime Academy predates the Cape Cod Canal, but the cadets of the academy have always lived by and loved Cape Cod Bay. Academy training ships traversed the bay twice each year as the cadets set sail on their annual sea term semester, excited to be out at sea on the outbound leg…and even more excited to be heading home on the return voyage. For the first fifty years of the academy's history, the training ships were sailing vessels with auxiliary steam power and the young boys aboard would scurry to the mast tops to catch the last (or first) sight of home. They were in training to become captains or chief engineers on the new steam-powered freighters and passenger liners of their day. The work was hard and the life was Spartan, but the rewards, both in responsibility and remuneration, were great.

For the last fifty years, the academy training ships have been huge steam-powered former freighters, now converted to floating college campuses with classrooms, dormitory and messing capability to take over five hundred young male and female students on a voyage of college education and discovery unlike any other. In a practice unchanged for over 117 years, those training ships, filled with the future, get underway. They now pass beneath the three latticework, Erector Set bridges that span the Cape Cod Canal and leave their temporary bright white scratch across the deep blue surface of Cape Cod Bay. And within minutes the bay erases the mark and returns to her former glory.

The sea surrounds us…and makes us glad.

Rick Gurnon
Rear Admiral, USMS
President, MMA

PREFACE

A historian should yield himself to his subject, become immersed in the place and period of his choice,
standing apart from it now and then for a fresh view.
—*Samuel Eliot Morison (1887–1976), U.S. historian noted for his works on American and maritime history*

The idea for this book arrived in bits and pieces in my imagination after years of independent historical research and my work in the field of contemporary marine public policy. It was sculpted to examine the depth and range of American society over several hundred years, and related cultures, as they pertain to the coastal embrace of Cape Cod Bay and how people used this ecosystem for food, economic sustenance, travel, warfare and other human actions. Where I could, I used primary materials for research, but I also leaned on secondary sources such as books. The last chapter examines contemporary issues that hinge yesteryear to tomorrow—topics future historians will analyze, from environmental public policy to cultural preservation.

This book is intended as a maritime history of Cape Cod Bay, not as a comprehensive history of this region of Massachusetts. I focus on select topics whose past engages the bay, including a review of the Pilgrim settlement in Plymouth and Native American relations with European settlers.

To that end, I am grateful to Saunders Robinson at The History Press, who supported the vision and concept of the book throughout the creative, research and composition processes, and I'm thankful for her faith, assistance and belief that this project could enrich and educate readers. Others at The History Press to whom I am grateful include Hilary McCullough, senior editor, who combed through the manuscript in her usual precise fashion, and Katie Parry and Dani McGrath, specialists in public relations and marketing, respectively, all of whom have been supportive with this project, and with my three preceding books.

I am indebted to the Dennis Historical Society, which granted permission for The History Press to use its oil painting depicting the *Searsville* for the cover of this book. And to Phyllis Horton, who provided information about the *Searsville*.

Mary Sicchio, special collections librarian at the William Brewster Nickerson Memorial Room at Cape Cod Community College, provided images for this book and shared documents in the research phase. Marcella Curry, a reference librarian at Sturgis

Library, steered me in the right direction on several occasions. Karin Goldstein, the reference librarian at Plimoth Plantation, assisted me in locating primary and secondary sources. Ria Convery, communications director at the Massachusetts Water Resource Authority, provided a graphic for this book. I am grateful to Steve McKenna of the Massachusetts Office of Coastal Zone Management (MA CZM) for the use of a map detailing Cape Cod Bay.

Duncan Oliver, a retired high school principal, historian/scholar and former president of the Historical Society of Old Yarmouth, shared his notes on Yarmouth's history, which I found valuable and instructive. Additionally, I relied on Duncan's book on shore whaling, composed with the late Jack Braginton-Smith. Bonnie and Stanley Snow of Orleans shared images from their extensive collection that were used in this book. Maureen Rukstalis of the Historical Society of Old Yarmouth also provided photographs. Historian Stauffer Miller shared his research on Cape Cod Civil War sea captains. Historians Jim Coogan of Sandwich and Mary Sicchio of Falmouth graciously served as readers. I am always thankful for extra sets of sharp eyes.

USMS Rear Admiral Richard Gurnon, president of the Massachusetts Maritime Academy, composed the foreword, which captures the spirit and dignity of Cape Cod Bay. Contributors of appendices were Gil Newton of Sandwich High School; Bill Burke of the Cape Cod National Seashore; Lisa Berry-Engler with the Massachusetts Office of Coastal Zone Management; Jeremy King, a fisheries biologist with the Massachusetts Division of Marine Fisheries; and Stormy Mayo, PhD, of the Provincetown Center for Coastal Studies.

Seth Rolbein, editor and publisher of *The Cape Cod Voice*, has my gratitude for granting permission to draw from select materials I researched and wrote from my years as history editor there from 2001 through 2004. Dan McKiernan, deputy director of Massachusetts Division of Marine Fisheries, insisted I read a chapter of a book about New England's fishing communities, and I'm glad I did.

Ian Mack of Orleans Camera in Dennis converted antique pictures into digital files for The History Press production team and has done so for my past three books.

I thank my family—my husband Dan and our children, Katherine and Thomas—for their support, good cheer and humor.

CHAPTER ONE

WHERE GEOLOGY MEETS
EARLY SCIENTIFIC RESEARCH

The Bay is so round and circling that before we could come to anchor we went around all the points of the compass. We could not come near the shore by three quarters of an English mile, because of shallow water which was a great prejudice to us, for our people going on shore were forced to wade a bow shoot or two in going a land which caused many to get colds and coughs, for it was many times freezing cold weather.
—Mourt's Relation

Cape Cod Bay's quintessential water sheet belies a vibrant ecosystem—a wealth of biodiversity—and is equally compelling for its place in the annals of American maritime and colonial history. At its geologic essence, "the reason we have a Cape Cod, and a Martha's Vineyard, and Nantucket, is because a glacier scraped the sand and gravel and silts and clays from north of here, and brought it here, and left it here," explained Graham Giese, PhD, director of the Land Sea Interaction Program at the Provincetown Center for Coastal Studies. Large "wind waves"—those waves being pushed along by strong, active winds, during a nor'easter, for example—from the northeast formed the early outer Cape shore and moved sediments to the south. At that time Georges Bank was a land mass, but over time it slowly sank as sea levels rose and it disappeared for good about six thousand years ago.

Ocean swells—waves that have outrun the wind—from the southeast began moving sediment to the north, forming the Provincetown hook. Veiled now from the eye by two hundred feet of salt water off Provincetown, mounds of sand are building on the ocean floor, continually adding to the hook.

Then, Giese said, wind waves from the northwest would have pushed sediments to the south, forming the early bayside of the outer Cape. "That process would have continued until the Provincetown hook—the fist and fingers of Cape Cod—grew out enough to protect the northernmost part of the bayside shore from those northwest wind waves."

The hook, or spit, is what shelters parts of Cape Cod Bay along the Truro shore from strong winter winds and the waves they produce. A land mass so "young" (by a geologist's reckoning) explains why agriculture isn't a primary occupation around these parts. The rest of New England draws its richness from antiquity. "We don't have much soil here because the glacial deposits are so recent…and that's not enough time for vegetation to produce a very thick soil," Giese added.

Twenty-five thousand years ago, the last monumental glacier called the Laurentide Ice Sheet retreated, according to radiocarbon results. (The Laurentide draws its name from the Laurentian region in Canada, where the sheet was originated.) Then, Cape Cod Bay was a lake, or a good part of it was. "This is the best known of all the glacial lakes because outwash deltas graded to the lake occur all around Cape Cod Bay from Duxbury to Truro," wrote Dr. Robert N. Oldale, a retired government geologist from Woods Hole. The majority of Cape Cod's landscape is composed of outwash plains, a melting pot of gravel and sand that streams deposited as they flowed in a braided pattern. "As the last continental ice sheets melted away, the water returned to the ocean basins and sea level rose," forming Cape Cod Bay, Oldale explained. "The remaining glacial landforms and the landforms created by the rise in sea level make up today's landscape," Oldale added.

Check the 3-D rendering of Stellwagen Bank for a full reckoning of the landforms once above ground: its underground terrain, which once saw daylight, and the marine life now supported there make it one of the most diverse marine ecological regions in the world.

Stellwagen Bank—the entry corridor to Massachusetts Bay—and Georges Bank used to be landforms, frequented by mastodons and other mammals. Stellwagen isn't technically in Cape Cod Bay. Because it's so nearby, any history of Cape Cod Bay would be remiss without mention of a prominent neighbor, the Stellwagen Bank National Marine Sanctuary.

On a crisp autumn day in October 1854, an ambitious U.S. Naval officer stood on the deck of a government steamship surveying and mapping shallow, offshore areas in Massachusetts Bay.

"I consider I have made an important discovery in the location of a 15 fathom bank lying in a line between Cape Cod and Cape Ann," wrote Lieutenant Commander Henry Schreiner Stellwagen to his boss, Alexander Bache at the U.S. Coast Survey, a forerunner to the National Oceanic and Atmospheric Administration (NOAA). In that letter, Stellwagen, a decorated career naval officer on loan to the coast survey, added details of his find. "We have traced nearly 5 miles in width and over 6 miles in length it no doubt extending much further."

It did. Stellwagen Bank—all 842 square miles of it—is the size of Rhode Island, and Stellwagen mapped it beginning in 1854. Stellwagen correctly deduced that his discovery was "essential to navigators, and that the knowledge of it will highly benefit commanders of vessels bound in during thick weather, by day or night."

Stellwagen devised a tool called the Stellwagen Cup—used for bringing up ocean bottom soil for testing—during his tenure with the U.S. Coast Survey, along with another device for measuring sea levels.

One of the most comprehensive studies in recent years on Cape Cod Bay was compiled by scientists at the Massachusetts Water Resource Authority (MWRA), which operates and monitors the Boston Effluent Tunnel, in operation since September 2000. Cape Cod Bay's currents flow counterclockwise. Following is an excerpt from the MWRA's seminal report depicting the seasonal cycles of Cape Cod Bay:

In November through April, winds and cooling mix the waters of the Bay. Nutrients are plentiful, but in December and January the penetration of light into the water is rarely enough to support the growth of phytoplankton (microscopic floating algae at the base of the food web). As the days lengthen in early spring, increases in light and in nutrient levels trigger the rapid growth of phytoplankton. The spring bloom of phytoplankton starts in the shallower waters of Cape Cod Bay, providing food for zooplankton (tiny animals, including juvenile forms of animals like fish and jellyfish, and abundant tiny crustaceans called copepods) carried into the Bay by strong currents from the Gulf of Maine. In turn, the fast-multiplying zooplankton provide food for many marine species including the northern right whale. A single right whale feeding in Cape Cod Bay can consume about one ton of these plankton daily. Later in the spring, the surface waters of the Bay warm and stratify. The phytoplankton grow abundantly at the surface, where they receive ample light. Because vertical mixing is prevented by stratification, the nutrients at the surface do not get replenished from the bottom waters. The phytoplankton use up the nutrients in the surface water and die, eventually sinking to the bottom and providing food to the bottom-dwelling animal communities which show a growth spurt in mid-summer. In the water column, bacteria use up dissolved oxygen through their respiration as they consume the dead plankton; the lowest dissolved oxygen levels in the Bay occur from August to October. In the fall, cooling of surface waters and strong winds allow mixing throughout the water column, bringing fresh nutrients to the surface, stimulating a new growth of phytoplankton—the fall bloom. By mid-winter, light levels have declined, ending the fall bloom. The plankton die and decay, releasing nutrients. Nutrient levels increase throughout the water column, preparing the Bay for the next spring bloom.

As far as anyone knows for certain, the first scientific readings of Cape Cod Bay were conducted in October 1789 by Jonathan Williams, a member of the prestigious American Philosophical Society in Philadelphia and nephew of Benjamin Franklin. In his landmark study, "Physical Oceanography of the Gulf of Maine," Henry Bigelow of Harvard University's Museum of Comparative Zoology and Woods Hole Oceanographic Institution reported that Williams read the "heat of the air and water at sunrise, noon, and sunset" on a voyage of exploration from Boston to Virginia. After 1850, which coincides with the end of the so-called Little Ice Age that cooled the earth between 1400 and 1800, Bigelow says the "entire gulf was colder than 50 degrees in March" 1870. Since then, the Gulf of Maine and Cape Cod Bay have been studied by private enterprises, nonprofit entities and government and university researchers.

Charting America's coastal waters became a priority for President Thomas Jefferson, and in 1807 he convinced Congress to pass the act entitled "The Survey of the Coast," the forerunner to today's National Oceanic and Atmospheric Administration (NOAA). "The Survey of the Coast charted the nation's ports and waterways, researched physical characteristics of the ocean bottom, and explored many of the world's oceans," according to a NOAA press release. In 2007, NOAA commemorated its 200th anniversary. Indeed, science was becoming a part of the American political infrastructure as early as Jefferson's time.

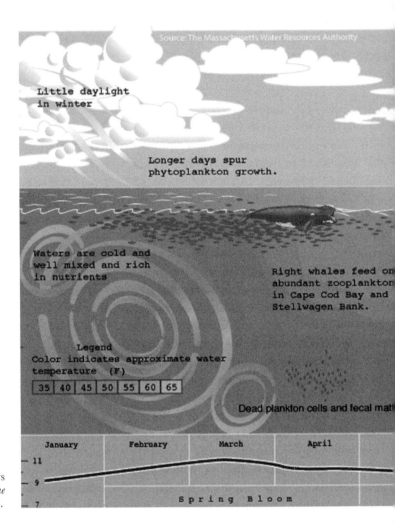

Source: The Massachusetts Water Resources Authority

Little daylight
in winter

Longer days spur
phytoplankton growth.

Waters are cold and
well mixed and rich
in nutrients

Right whales feed on
abundant zooplankton
in Cape Cod Bay and
Stellwagen Bank.

Legend
Color indicates approximate water
temperature (F)

| 35 | 40 | 45 | 50 | 55 | 60 | 65 |

Dead plankton cells and fecal matt

| January | February | March | April |

— 11

— 9

— 7

Spring Bloom

Water in Cape Cod Bay flows counterclockwise. *Courtesy of the Massachusetts Water Resource Authority.*

In July 1920, Albert Perry Brigham of Colgate University composed a research paper "Cape Cod and the Old Colony" for the *Geographical Review*. Brigham read his paper before the Association of American Geographers, which met in St. Louis. His work specialized in "human geography," as Brigham himself put it, with attention paid to the first permanent white settlers who established colonies and later towns along Cape Cod Bay: "Though the Pilgrims did not come to fish or to sail, they were forced to do both by their marine environment," asserted Brigham. He wrote about the smallest of waterways that connected communities to Cape Cod Bay. "The grist mill was imperative, and within a few years of the *Mayflower* mills were built at Plymouth, and then, to save long and laborious journeys, at Sandwich. Surface streams with suitable fall are so rare on the Cape that wind power was invoked, and the windmill became a common object in the landscape."

Going strictly by the numbers, Cape Cod Bay measures about 604 statute square miles in a line drawn between Race Point in Provincetown and Brant Rock in Marshfield. Within those fifteen towns are no fewer than fifteen harbors, just under ten rivers, a

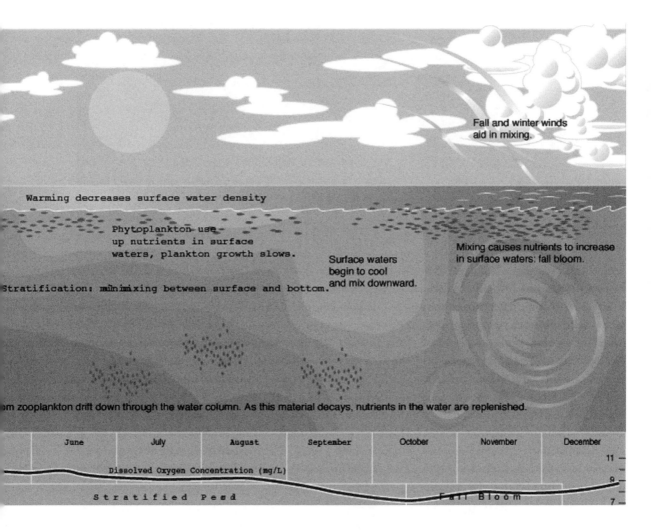

Fall and winter winds aid in mixing.

Warming decreases surface water density

Phytoplankton use up nutrients in surface waters, plankton growth slows.

Surface waters begin to cool and mix downward.

Mixing causes nutrients to increase in surface waters: fall bloom.

Stratification: minimixing between surface and bottom.

om zooplankton drift down through the water column. As this material decays, nutrients in the water are replenished.

| June | July | August | September | October | November | December |

Dissolved Oxygen Concentration (mg/L)

11

9

Stratified Pead

Fall Bloom

7

handful of creeks and several coves, a few brooks, two energy power plants and, lest we forget, one huge canal. Put in a larger context, Cape Cod Bay forms the southernmost reach of the Gulf of Maine, with the Bay of Fundy forming its northern boundary.

Cape Cod Bay is about two hundred feet deep at its deepest point, though its average depth is about eighty feet.

> *Cape Cod Bay is recognized as an important resource statewide and nationally. In 1974, the Massachusetts Oceans Sanctuaries Act recognized Cape Cod Bay as an important ocean sanctuary. Four state-recognized Areas of Critical Environmental Concern are within Cape Cod Bay. In 1995, Cape Cod Bay was designated an Estuary of National Significance as part of the Massachusetts Bays Program. Cape Cod Bay also contains a federally designated Critical Habit for rare and endangered species. Cape Cod Bay has over 390 public beaches and there are an estimated 400,000 acres of shellfish-growing areas between Provincetown and the Back River in Hull.*
>
> *—Environmental Protection Agency, Region 1, June 2008*

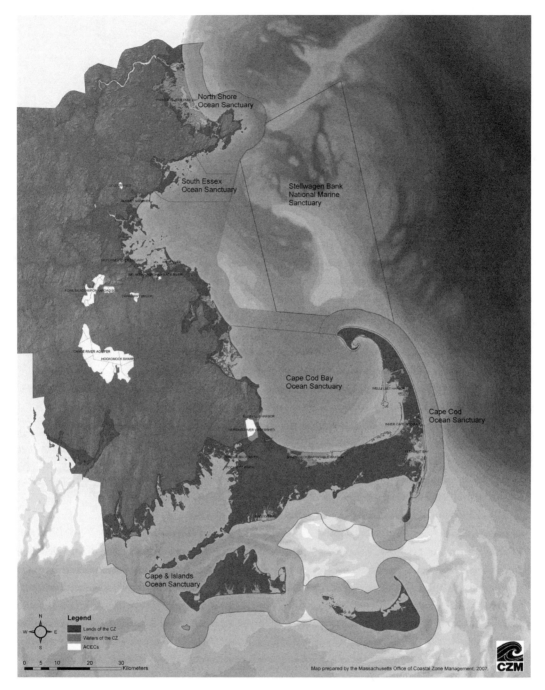

Cape Cod Bay is a State Ocean Sanctuary. *Courtesy of the Massachusetts Office of Coastal Zone Management.*

CHAPTER TWO

PEOPLE OF THE FIRST LIGHT

He was a patriot attached to his native soil—a prince true to his subjects, and indignant of their wrongs—a soldier, daring in battle, firm in adversity, patient of fatigue, of hunger, of every variety of bodily suffering, and ready to perish in the cause he had espoused.
—*Washington Irving describing Metacom, or King Philip*

The Wampanoag call themselves the People of the First Light, since the morning sun touches their ancestral lands first before sweeping west across the country. Here they lived for centuries, untouched by cultures other than Native American. The Wampanoag and members of other tribes established villages throughout contemporary Barnstable County and, indeed, throughout New England, including modern-day Plymouth, which they called Patuxet. Ancestral native names grace street signs and post offices and have become an integral part of communal life along Cape Cod Bay.

How many generations of Wampanoag lived in this region will never be known, but based on archaeological data, the native people may have been here at least twelve thousand years. After glaciers receded and the bays, rivers, ponds and estuaries stabilized, Native Americans established permanent and seasonal settlements. These included the Aquetnet at Skauton Neck (modern-day Scorton Neck on Cape Cod Bay); Cummaquid at Barnstable Harbor; Mattakees or Mattakeset in today's Barnstable and Yarmouth towns; the Meeshawn in Provincetown; the Nauset near Eastham; Nemskaket in Orleans; Nobsqussit or Nobscusset in Dennis; the Pamet near Truro; and Sawkatuket or Satucket in Brewster.

The change and rhythms of seasons marked patterns for this small, fledging civilization. In spring, herring, among other food sources, fed the people. Herring was used as fertilizer, too. The riches of land sustained these tribes. Many of the foods we eat today originated among native people, including tribes around Cape Cod Bay: blackberries, blueberries, cranberries, wild game including turkey, crabs, clam chowder, lobsters and bean soup. Maize (Indian corn) and kidney beans was a staple native meal. Into this pottage went fresh or dried fish and meat like beaver or bear, eaten off wooden dishes and spoons.

Hartman Deetz is a member of the Wampanoag tribe and cultural researcher who used to work as an interpreter at Plimoth Plantation's Native American settlement. What follows are key excerpts in his own words:

A village would spread out along the water's edge, where generations of land management would have left a mile or so clear of trees. Women were responsible for the planting and gathering of wild fruits, nuts, greens and vegetables, as well as shellfish. Men would be active in one of the most important harvests of the year—taking herring. Also, other types of fish were taken as well, as hook line and sinker systems were employed, as were net, spears and baited basket traps. Fish weirs were particularly important as well. An area of about two acres in Boston's Back Bay yielded 65,000 posts for a massive fish weir system that would have been used as a common property location for many communities to come and take advantage of.

Native Americans lived within nuclear family units in small homes. Each clan had about three acres, surrounded by corn, with private fields abutting one another along the coast. "It would be impossible to tell where one community ended and the next began," Deetz claimed. "Families would remain spread out in their planting homes through the summer and into the fall," he added. "During the summer all protein came from fish supplemented by fresh fruits, vegetables and greens." Natives grew apples and made cider, but water was their primary drink.

"Their houses, or wigwams, are built with small poles fixed in the ground, bent and fastened together with barks of trees oval or arbour-wise on the top," wrote Daniel Gookin in *Historical Collections of the Indians of New England*. Some homes were larger than others based on the size of the family, the structure's purpose and how much activity was centered there. "Some I have seen of sixty or a hundred feet long, and thirty feet broad," added Gookin.

Many species of fish were smoked for winter consumption. Marine fare was the core of native diets in the summer, according to Deetz:

The standard boat for coastal people was the mishoon (dugout canoe) some measuring up to 60 feet wide and 60 feet long, operated by a crew of about 40 men. With these vessels sturgeon, tuna and pilot whales were taken from the deep waters, as well as trade conducted over water. Wampanoag people would travel as far north as Nova Scotia and as far south as the Chesapeake Bay. Birch bark canoes were used to travel inland waterways as far as Niagra Falls. Throughout this area the various tribal nations were all of a common cultural/linguistic group of the Algonquin Nation…with similar customs of education, spiritual beliefs and governance. This made trade easy, and often times long-term trade agreements and military alliances were formed over the water, including, most presumably, on Cape Cod Bay.

In fall, the Wampanoag would leave their planting homes to resettle into central villages between one and five miles from the coast of Cape Cod Bay. The forests afforded protection from nor'easters and the daily wet, cold winds. Deetz clarified:

Whole clans would live under one roof in large bark-covered homes, and in some villages the population would surpass 3,000. As well as sheltering Native people from the wintertime North Atlantic, the forest would provide wood for fires and game for hunting.

Fowl were taken in the spring and the fall but mammals were only taken after first frost and until the return to the coast. Fish smoked in the warm weather as well as sun-dried vegetables would supplement the diet through the winter, but some ice fishing was done, as well as eel, which was easier to obtain in the winter.

And the land cured them, too. Native tribes in New England and along Cape Cod Bay did not know infectious or contagious diseases until the white explorers arrived. Old World deadly and serious diseases, such as smallpox, diphtheria, and the bubonic plague, were simply unknown. [Syphilis, thought to have been brought by Europeans, might have actually been derived from yaws, a chronic skin disease common in warm climes.] Plant extracts played a major role for native people who complained about toothaches or injuries sustained during warfare or hunting and all manner of sores, aches and pains. The range of native pharmacopoeia is staggering. The root of the wild blackberry soothed a sore throat. To stop bleeding, a spider's web was applied to a wound. To get rid of a headache, inhaling the fumes of heated red cedar leaves worked well. Howard S. Russell writes in *Indian New England Before the Mayflower* of the seemingly endless variety of native cures for digestive troubles: "Goose or skunk oil, or a purgative of butternut bark, would clear the bowels; columbine root or cattail flowers ended diarrhea; a cedar leaf concoction relieved dropsy and urinary difficulties."

Weaving and sewing were left to the women. Men hunted and repaired tools and household items, including spoons and bowls. "Extended family and community were reinforced in the winter as it was easy to come together and discuss politics," insisted Deetz. "Elders would pass stories on to the next generation. Young cousins played together and shared the company of those that called the village home." The cycle would repeat itself year after year, especially in spring, when herring returned to marine estuaries, rivers and inlets connected to Cape Cod Bay.

Wampanoag along Cape Cod Bay were largely peaceful and "gregarious," in the words of one seventeenth-century eyewitness. "A pleasanter characteristic of the Cape Cod Indians was their amazing friendliness to the white men—at first to those fleeting voyagers to the Cape shores, and afterwards to the permanent settlers there," wrote Henry Kittredge in his seminal tome *Cape Cod: Its People and Their History*.

Squanto, who also went by the native name of Tisquantum, is famous for his role in procuring food for the Pilgrims and, according to Kittredge, helping to locate the "worthless youngster named John Billington, who was always in trouble and who this time got lost in the woods," separated from his family and the rest of the *Mayflower* passengers.

In the winter of 1631, the tribe came to the rescue of colonists run aground in a storm. A Boston merchant and cobbler, Richard Garrett, sailed in January for Plymouth with his daughter and a crew of four men. A northerly gale blew the small vessel across Cape Cod Bay. They came ashore somewhere near present-day Barnstable. Two of the men started on foot for Plymouth and on the way the pair met two Indians, one of whom went along with them, while the other went back to help those who had stayed with the boat. He found them almost frozen, built a shelter over them and started a fire to thaw them out. Garrett died. The Wampanoag native used his tomahawk to chop a grave into the frozen ground, and laid Garrett to rest there. Garrett's daughter and one of the men survived. The two who had started for Plymouth died—one at the Manomet trading post and the other on arriving at Plymouth, according to Kittredge.

Decades later, King Philip's War, also known as Metacom's War, broke out and the conflict from 1675 to 1676 was between Native Americans and English colonists and their native allies. It was one of the bloodiest wars in American warfare, and one of the lesser known. Over fifty New England communities were attacked, including Plymouth, but the war did not extend to Cape Cod, and the Wampanoag people largely stayed neutral in the conflict. Metacom, or King Philip, was a son of Massasoit, the powerful sachem of the Wampanoag, once a strong ally to Plymouth colonists.

One of the best interpretations of the conflict was coauthored by Eric B. Schultz and Michael J. Tougias in *King Philip's War: The History and Legacy of America's Forgotten War*:

> *The war erupted on June 20, 1657, along the southern border of Plymouth Colony, and it is startling to see how quickly two peoples, having lived side by side for a half century, could become consumed so quickly and completely with an intense hatred for one another. A small band of Pokanoket (a people of Wampanoag) warriors left their camp in present-day Warren, Rhode Island, crossed the Kickamuit River, and raided several farms in the English settlement at Swansea. A messenger was immediately dispatched to Governor Josiah Winslow at Marshfield, who on June 22 sent orders to Bridgewater and Taunton to raise a force of two hundred men for the defense of Plymouth Colony's frontier.*
>
> *Three days after the raid, twenty-year-old John Salisbury of Swansea shot and mortally wounded a marauding Pokanoket. Within a day Pokanoket warriors had ambushed and killed seven English, leaving the entire Swansea settlement of about forty families huddled in three or four secure garrisons.*

Philip was later cornered, shot and killed by John Alderman, an Indian, on August 12, 1676. His head was cut off and posted at Plymouth for nearly two decades. The war decimated native populations and effectively ended the way native tribes sustained themselves and their culture. Schultz and Tougias reported that the yearlong war was costly:

> *Between six hundred and eight hundred English died in battle during King Philip's War. Measured against a European population in New England of perhaps fifty-two thousand, this death rate was nearly twice that of the Civil War and more than seven times that of World War II.*

Most natives who survived the conflict suffered greatly. Their way of life was gone forever. The colonial government sold many into slavery in the West Indies and allowed select few Praying Indians to migrate to other established Christian Indian settlements in New England. Many were forced under guard and shackles onto Deer Island and other small islands that today compose the Boston Harbor Islands National Recreation Area. Eventually exposure, starvation and lack of medical care caused the deaths of nearly half the native prisoners there.

The Cape Cod Wampanoag continued on with their quiet lives.

CHAPTER THREE

EUROPEANS WASH ASHORE

Men go abroad to wonder at the heights of mountains, at the huge waves of the sea, at the long courses of the rivers, at the vast compass of the ocean, at the circular motions of the stars, and they pass by themselves without wondering.
—Saint Augustine

One by one, ship by ship, Europeans arrived along the eastern seaboard. Their goals varied. Some explored to claim new territories on behalf of their rulers, and others wished to permanently settle elsewhere for political, religious or economic reasons, or all of the above. As white Europeans sailed through, across and into Cape Cod Bay, the communities that the native people had constructed would change forever.

According to Editor Simeon Deyo in his seminal late nineteenth-century history of Cape Cod, the "famous Verrazano map of 1529, prepared by James Verrazano, tracing the discoveries of John Verrazano, appears for the first time upon any chart of the New World an outline of the coast of the present Cape Cod, sufficiently distinct for identification. The claim of John Verrazano as the first discoverer of Cape Cod is established by the Verrazano chart, and fifty years ago or more would, perhaps, have been undisputed."

Deyo insists, based on historical records, that a handful of lesser-known explorers briefly skirted Cape Cod Bay after Verrazano's arrival:

> *The transitions in nomenclature that appear upon the charts of the fifteenth and sixteenth centuries afford an idea of the history of Cape Cod during the years that intervened between the voyage of Verrazano and the landing of the Pilgrims. Upon a chart of Ribero published in 1529 Cape Cod appears as* C. de Arenas *or Sandy cape, a name that recurs upon the map of Rotz in 1542; Mercator, 1569; Judeis, 1580; and Quadus, 1600, indicating, perhaps, that the soil of the Cape has not changed materially with the lapse of time. Another Rotz chart of 1542 gives to the Cape the title Arecifes, while a chart of Jean Allefonsce, who visited Massachusetts in 1557, uses the name Francescan cape to designate the* Cabo de los Arenas *of the earlier maps. Of the details of these voyages, the record of which the early charts alone preserve, nothing is now known. The early navigators, however, uniformly applied the name Cape to that portion of Cape Cod*

lying northerly of High Head in Truro, and doubtless seldom sailed along the eastern coast of the United States without passing in sight of the headland, the glittering sands of which so early acquired the name of Sandy cape.

The "Viking question" is best answered this way: so little data are known, or wickedly surmised. Simply put, no one is proof-positive that Vikings were here, though no one can refute that Norsemen sailed in the western North Atlantic, if ancient Norse texts and maps are to be believed.

In his book *New England's Viking and Indian Wars*, Robert Ellis Cahill writes that Leif Ericson, a son of Eric the Red, was the teenage captain of a 1,800-mile nonstop voyage to the south, presumably to what is now called Cape Cod. Researchers surmise Ericson must have reached the Cape. This is based solely on vague geographic descriptions passed down from Norse legend. Their voyage was described by them as "a most beautiful land with wonderful white sand," and they sailed "through the sound which lay between the island and that cape, which projected northward from the land itself." None can be certain that Cape Cod Bay was actually visited by young Ericson.

He was a methodical man, not prone to whimsy, a thorough sailor who planned his actions well. Captain Bartholomew Gosnold had his sights set on exploring the New World for England's glory, and sought passages to facilitate commercial marine markets. His vessel, the *Concord*, sailed into Cape Cod Bay on Saturday, May 15, 1602. "Like a stallion corralled, the *Concord* sailed first to the east then to the west along the southern shore of Cape Cod Bay, looking for a way to escape through the encircling arm of the Cape to more southerly waters beyond," wrote Warner F. Gookin and Phillip Barbour, coauthors of *Bartholomew Gosnold—Discoverer and Planter*. Gosnold was the first English explorer to sail into Cape Cod Bay.

A short time later, Gosnold stepped ashore on present-day Barnstable. First Mate John Brereton's account of the landing includes:

> [We] *went ashore, being a white sandie and very bolde shore; and marching all that afternoon with our musket on our necks, on the highest hills which we saw (the weather was very hot) at length we perceived this headland to be a parcell of the maine…we espied an Indian, a yong man, of proper stature, and of a pleasing countenance; and after some familiarities with him, we left him at the sea side, and returned to our ship, where, in fiue or sixe houres absence, we had pestered our ship with Cod fish, that we threw numbers of them ouer-boord againe.*

Gookin, a retired minister who dedicated the last of his years to compiling known data about Gosnold, wrote:

> *Five days later, on Friday, May 21, Gosnold was again coasting along a shore of Cape Cod. But this time he was in the quiet waters of Nantucket Sound on his way to his most notable discoveries, searching for a southern entrance to the sound. Others had seen Cape Cod from a distance, before Bartholomew Gosnold stepped ashore in 1602. Cabot had*

sailed down the coast from Newfoundland in 1498, perhaps as far as Cape Hatteras, claiming everything in sight for the King of England. Following him in ever-increasing numbers, Spanish, Portuguese and French vessels sailed up and down, some exploring, some on voyages to the Newfoundland fisheries. By 1600, Captain Edward Hayes reported 400 ships yearly were visiting the fisheries, a large proportion of them undoubtedly fishermen from Southern Europe who had crossed the tropics to Florida and then coasted up to Newfoundland. All these coasting vessels must have passed Cape Cod not far off shore, but only one of them has any semblance of a claim to having discovered it.

A year after Gosnold's trip, Captain Martin Pring arrived and spent six weeks in Plymouth Harbor "loading sassafras," a spice highly prized in Europe for its medicinal value. Pring, according to Howard S. Russell, ate "Pease and Beanes" with the natives and watched them dance to the tune of a zittern a sailor played. Pring wrote of seeing "faire big strawberries" and other fruits cultivated by the Wampanoag. "On another occasion, the men harvesting sassafras were taking their usual two hour siesta in the woods when more than a hundred Indians armed with bows and arrows appeared," wrote Richard F. Whalen in *Truro: The Story of a Cape Cod Town*. "They surrounded the stockade and called to the four guards to come out, but the men refused. Captain Pring, alone with two men on his ship, became alarmed and fired a cannon to scare the Indians and waken the men sleeping in the woods. It took a second shot to bring his men to their feet. They picked up their weapons and let loose the mastiffs." In Pring's journal, he writes that the Indians "turned all to a jest and sport, and departed away in a friendly manner."

In 1604, the French sponsored a trip to New England for Samuel de Champlain, whose log included this entry:

The White Cape is a point of sand which bends southward some six leagues. This Coast has fairly high sand-banks which are very conspicuous from the sea, where Soundings are found of thirty, forty and fifty fathoms nearly fifteen or eighteen leagues from land, until one comes to ten fathoms in approaching the shore, which is very clear. There is a great extend of open country along the shore before one enters the woods, which are very delightful and pleasant to the eye. We can anchor off shore and saw some Indians, towards whom four of our party advanced. Making their way along the sandy beach, they perceived as it were a bay with wigwams bordering it all around.

Champlain composed a precise map of Plymouth Harbor and Russell noted that Champlain pictured "the shore of the bay as largely cleared except for scattered trees."

In 1613, Adrian Block explored Cape Cod, sailing north from New Amsterdam "to claim the Cape for the Dutch. The name 'Staten hoeck' appears by Cape Cod on Dutch maps of 1614 and 1635," according to a report entitled "Historic Archaeological Services" by UMass of Amherst, in cooperation with the National Park Service (NPS).

Captain John Smith

In spring 1614, Captain John Smith sailed to New England. His journals, published several years later, describe a raw country—wood and water—and he claimed the region for Prince Charles of England. First Smith visited lands to the north and then made his way to Cape Cod Bay. He described the shore as "onely a headland of high hils of sand, ouergrowne with shrubbie pines…but an excellent harbor for all weathers. This Cape is made by the maine Sea on the one side, and a great Bay on the other in forme of a fickle: on it doth inhabit the people of Pawmet: and in the bottome of the Bay, the people of Chawum."

Captain Smith, noted Howard S. Russell in *Indian New England Before the Mayflower*, surveyed the entire Massachusetts Bay and Boston Harbor, and said he "counted forty villages between Cape Cod and Penobscot Bay."

Thomas Hunt

One man severely damaged fledging relations with Native Americans who lived among the land, marshes, dunes and forests around Cape Cod Bay: explorer Thomas Hunt. When John Smith departed local waters, he left Hunt behind to gather dried fish. "Hunt not only gathered codfish but also kidnapped and enslaved Native Americans, including Tisquantum, or Squanto, at Patuxet (what is now Plymouth)," according to the UMass-NPS report. More about this incident appears in *Mourt's Relation*, from a Pilgrim entry dated June 11, 1622, near present-day Eastham:

> *One thing was very grevious to us at this place. There was an old woman whom we judged to be no less than a hundred years old, which came to see us because she never saw English, yet could not behold us without breaking forth into great passion, weeping and crying excessively. We demanding the reason of it, they told us she had three sons who, when Master Hunt was in these parts, went aboard his ship to trade with him, and he carried them captives into Spain (for Squanto at that time was carried away also) by which means she was deprived of the comfort of her children in her old age. We told them we were sorry that any Englishman should give them that offense, that Hunt was a bad man, and that all the English that heard of it condemned him for the same; but for us, we would not offer them any injury though it would gain us all the skins in the country. So we gave her small trifles which somewhat appeased her.*

Hunt kidnapped twenty-seven natives, but Squanto was later returned to America and would prove invaluable to the Mayflower Company. Various accounts differ on the eventual fate of the other captives. For decades to come, a combination of goodwill and animosity existed between Europeans and natives along Cape Cod Bay until the end of King Philip's War. Five years after Thomas Hunt sailed away from Plymouth, the Separatists arrived. We would begin referring to the *Mayflower* passengers as Pilgrims in the nineteenth century.

John Josselyn

Natural historian, poet and traveler John Josselyn of England sailed along the eastern seaboard and composed two books, including *An Account of Two Voyages to New-England*. It is said that "Josselyn's contributions to early American culture have been undervalued," according to Editor Paul J. Lindholdt, who studied Josselyn's works and published his findings in 1988.

In 1674, Josselyn sailed into Cape Cod Bay:

> *Doubling the Cape we came into the great Bay, on the West thereof is New-Plimoth-Bay, on the Southwest-end of this Bay is situated New-Plimouth, the first English-Colony that took firm possession in this Countrey, which was in 1620, and the first Town built therein, whose longitude is 315 degrees, in latitude 41 degrees and 37 minutes, it was built nine years before any other Town, from the beginning of it to 1669 is just forty years, in which time there Hath been an increasing of forty Churches in this Colony.*

CHAPTER FOUR

PERMANENCE ON CAPE COD BAY

That same day, so soon as we could we set ashore fifteen or sixteen men, well armed, with some to fetch wood, for we had none left; as also to see what the land was, an what inhabitants they could meet with.
—Governor William Bradford, aboard the Mayflower *in November 1620*

The Saints and Strangers Arrive

The Saints, as the religious *Mayflower* passengers were called, became the first white settlers along Cape Cod Bay. Cold and exhausted, the *Mayflower* sailed into Cape Cod Bay where Bartholomew Gosnold had visited eighteen years before. Governor William Bradford's account provides the well-known narrative:

> *After longe beating at sea they fell with that land which is called Cape Cod; the which being made & certainly knowne to be it, they were not a little joyfull. After some deliberation had amongst them selves & with ye mr. of ye ship, they tacked aboute and resolved to stande for ye southward (ye wind & weather being faire) to finde some place aboute Hudsons river* [location uncertain] *for their habitation. But after they sailed Yt course aboute halfe ye day, they fell amongst deangerous shoals and roring breakers, and they were so farr intangled ther with as they conceived them selves in great danger; & ye wind shrinking upon them withal, they get out of those dangers before nigh overtook them, as by Gods providence they did. And ye next day they got into the Cape-harbor wher they ridd in saftie. A word of too by ye way of this cape; it was thus first named by Capten Gosnole & his company (because yey tooke much of yt fishe there), Ano: 1602, and after by Capten Smith was caled Cape James; but it retains Ye former name amongst seamen...*
>
> *Being thus arived in a good harbor and brought safe to land, they fell Upon their knees & blessed ye God of heaven, who had brought them over Ye vast & furious ocean, and delivered them from all ye periles & miseries thereof, againe to set their feete on ye firme and stable earth, their proper elemente.*

Within days, the Mayflower Company signed the famous Mayflower Compact in Provincetown Harbor in Cape Cod Bay on November 11, 1620. It remains the first democratic document signed in the New World:

> *In the name of God, Amen. We whose names are under-written, the loyal subjects of our dread sovereign Lord, King James, by the grace of God, of Great Britain, France, and Ireland King, Defender of the Faith, etc.*
>
> *Having undertaken, for the glory of God, and advancement of the Christian faith, and honor of our King and Country, a voyage to plant the first colony in the northern parts of Virginia, do by these presents solemnly and mutually, in the presence of God, and one of another, covenant and combine our selves together into a civil body politic, for our better ordering and preservation and furtherance of the ends aforesaid; and by virtue hereof to enact, constitute, and frame such just and equal laws, ordinances, acts, constitutions and offices, from time to time, as shall be thought most meet and convenient for the general good of the Colony, unto which we promise all due submission and obedience. In witness whereof we have hereunder subscribed our names at Cape Cod, the eleventh of November [New Style, November 21], in the year of the reign of our sovereign lord, King James, of England, France, and Ireland, the eighteenth, and of Scotland the fifty-fourth. Anno Dom. 1620.*

Historian Nathaniel Philbrick wrote, "Given the future course of New England and the United States, there is a temptation to make more out of the Mayflower Compact than there actually was. In truth, the compact made no attempt to propose that they now alter the form of government that existed in any town back in England. What made the document truly extraordinary was that it applied to a group of people who were three thousand miles from their mother country."

Staid religious beliefs failed to conceal boisterous personalities. Stephen Hopkins was often drunk, sneaked shuffleboard games in on the Sabbath and physically whipped *Mayflower* passenger John Tisdale after the two argued. Hopkins, a tanner by trade, served as an ambassador to Native Americans and eased the transition strains for the *Mayflower* passengers. He had made an earlier voyage to the New World aboard the Virginia-bound *Sea Venture* in 1609, which was wrecked in a storm off Bermuda. Hopkins eventually made it to Jamestown, where he stayed for two years before returning to England.

William Brewster, on the other hand, was the antithesis of Hopkins. He was that idealized Pilgrim whose serene image is embossed in America's quintessential dream of Pilgrim purity. Educated at Cambridge University, Brewster served as postmaster, a prestigious position in his native Nottinghamshire, England. As a leader in the Separatist movement, he proved a quiet leader and a force in the publishing of illegal religious materials that inspired the Pilgrims to leave Holland for America.

While the only thing these two men had in common was a one-way ticket on the *Mayflower*, Hopkins and Brewster share the distinction of being fellow signers of the Mayflower Compact.

Exploring New Shores

With the *Mayflower* anchored in present-day Provincetown Harbor and the passengers eager to explore, a small boat was launched with about fifteen men to survey the shore of Cape Cod Bay and replenish stores of firewood. According to *Mourt's Relation*, the *Mayflower* passengers embraced their new surroundings. "On this side where we lay is the bay, and the further side the sea; the ground or earth, sand hills, much like the downs in Holland, but much better; the crust of the earth's a spit's depth excellent black earth; all wooded with oaks, pines, sassafras, juniper, birch, holly, vines, some ash, walnut; the wood for the most part open and without underwood, fit either to go or ride in."

In the days ahead along the shore of Cape Cod Bay, the *Mayflower* explorers would find a cache of Indian corn, repair a small boat and take an informal panorama of the natural wonders—the wild geese, ducks and wildlife, including deer—along the bay's wooded areas. Signs of Indian occupation included native double-matted houses. "In the houses we found wooden bowls, trays and dishes, earthen pots, handbaskets made of crabshells wrought together, also an English pail or bucket; it wanted a bail, but it had two iron ears," reads *Mourt's Relation*.

In early December, a shore expedition ended with an angry exchange with Natives, the so-called First Encounter. Around 5:00 a.m., one of the *Mayflower* men cried out, "They are men! Indians! Indians! And withal, their arrows came flying amongst us. Our men ran out with all speed to recover their arms, as by the good providence of God they did," recounted *Mourt's*. The quick flurry ended quickly with no one on either side wounded by arrow or musket ball. Later that day, the shallop full of explorers ended up in Plymouth Harbor. A few days later, the shallop crew returned to Provincetown Harbor for the *Mayflower*, which then sailed across Cape Cod Bay to Plymouth.

Retrieving the lost boy, John Billington, took English colonists out on the water sheet. In the venerable tome *Of Plymouth Plantation*, Governor William Bradford wrote, "About the latter end of this month, one John Billington lost himself in the woods, and wandered up and down some five days, living on berries and what he could find." Young Billington wandered into an Indian settlement at Manomet, and those natives met up at the "Yarmouth flats" at Cummaquid to "trade good will with the Indians for return of a lost boy," according to Haynes Mahoney in *Yarmouth's Proud Packets*. "The Cummaquid clan proved helpful, the boy was found and in the course of the proceedings, the Pilgrims established friendly relations with Sachem Iyannough and his tribe, returning on various trips to trade for corn and beans. It could be said to be the beginning of maritime commerce between Cape Cod and the mainland," added Mahoney.

Aptucxet Trading Post, Bourne: America's First Business Enterprise

The Pilgrims were businessmen who farmed to sustain themselves and their families. In the New World, the natural resources hugging Cape Cod Bay, from fish to fur, seemed inexhaustible, making trade king. In 1627 the Pilgrims "discovered Buzzards Bay and

Manomet River, and they discovered the short passage between, and that meant they didn't have to go around the Cape, so they built the trading post to build their goods there," clarified Eleanor Hammond, site manager for the Bourne Historical Society. The Wampanoag named the Manomet River, which means "trail of the burden carriers." A dedicated scholar over two decades, Ms. Hammond said the post was a good twenty-three miles on foot through the woods from Plymouth, and indentured servants maintained the post.

"It was the first free commercial enterprise in the New World," explained Hammond. "They developed the first money system, the whole economic beginning of American enterprise," she added. The English traded sassafras root, tobacco from Virginia, clay beads and woolen cloth. The Indians, however, wouldn't buy the clay beads from the Pilgrims because the Dutch had much better quality beads. Through trading at Aptucxet, wampum—the rare purple part of the quahog shell—became a legitimate form of currency and marked the "first time it became used as money," Hammond clarified. "The white beads of quahogs could be any color...plenty of white shells which were used. When it came to the purple, that was the only one in North America suitable for the purple bead," she explained.

Aptucxet was the only trading post in operation at that time. The Boston Trading Post was not established until 1630. A second trading post was constructed by Pilgrims in Maine, and in 1633 a third was added in Connecticut; businessmen traveled to these posts by foot or by canoe. Pinnace or shallops (sloops) were also used for long coastal trading trips, and trading partners at Aptucxet included the Dutch who hailed from New Amsterdam, present-day Manhattan.

Distinguished Visitors to Plymouth

John Pory

Cape Cod Bay might also bear the lesser distinction of being the first site of a marine business trip. In 1622, John Pory (1572–1635) visited Plymouth aboard the *Discovery* following a three-year tour of duty as secretary to the governor and council of Virginia. Educated and portly, friendly, restless and with a taste for wine, Pory enjoyed his travels. Indeed, he was no novice in that area. Turkey, Greece, France, Italy and Ireland were included in his state missions.

In a letter to the Earl of Southampton dated January 13, 1622, Pory mentioned Cape Cod Bay, having arrived there by accident due to a less than capable pilot who originally aimed the ship for Cape Ann. "Arriving at that stately harbor called Cape Cod, called by Indians 'Pamet'...after some dangerous and almost incurable errors and mistaking, he stumbled by accident upon the harbour of Plymouth."

"First, the harbour is not only pleasant for air and prospect, but most sure for shipping, both small and great, being land-locked on all sides." Had the term "biodiversity" been in use in 1622, it would have fit the bill perfectly, given Pory's description of Cape Cod Bay as "no place in the world that can match it." Clearly Cape Cod Bay and its culinary potential impressed Pory: eels pouring forth in March and "plenty of fish and fowl every day in the year." In spring, schools of herring "or old wives" formed which Pory saw "running under the town, and so into a great pond or lake of a mile broad, where they cast their spawn, the water of the said river being in many places not above half a foot deep." Pory witnessed the seines—a form of gentle fishing—of bass and bluefish about mid-May. "Some fishes of a foot and a half, some of two foot, and some of three foot long, and with hooks, those of four and five feet long."

Pory developed a culinary fondness for bluefish "and of a taste requiring no addition of sauce. By which alluring qualities it may seem dangerously tending to a surfeit, but we found by experience that having satisfied (and in a manner glutted) ourselves therewith, it proved wholesome unto us and most easy of digestion."

Lobsters proved all the rage. "So large, so full of meat, and so plentiful in number as no man will believe that hath not seen. For a price of three halfpence, I bought ten lobsters that would well have dined forty laboring men," Pory wrote. He said even the cabin boy aboard the *Discovery* dined well on the crustaceans. The diplomat said Cape Codders enjoyed "muscles and slammes [clams] all the year long." Twenty miles up the coast of Cape Cod Bay, Pory reported that "savages" talk of "such huge" oysters being plentiful. Cape Cod Bay, he reported, "is covered with all sorts of water fowl, in such sort of swarms and multitudes as is rather admirable than credible."

It would appear that Pory ate his way through the Plymouth Colony.

In his letter to Southampton, Pory's observations touched on colonists' relations with Native American tribes. "They are friends with all their neighbors—as namely with those of Cohasset and Massachusetts to the north, with the great kind of Pocanocket to the southwest, with those of Pamet, Nauset, Capawack and others to the east and south."

Pory visited New England "to get the company firsthand information about the fishing business in New England, see what the Council for New England was actually doing, and assess the prospects of the Plymouth settlement," according to Sydney V. James Jr., who edited Pory's letters in *Three Visitors to Early Plymouth*.

Emmanuel Altham

Because Emmanuel Altham was born a third son to an English gentleman, he did not inherit family property at Mark Hall, Latton, just north of London. Altham made his own way into the world of international commerce, first as an investor in the Company of Adventurers for New Plymouth and later as an agent. "He went to the New World with a sense of honor, moreover, rather than the qualities of a hard-driving trader," wrote Sydney V. James Jr. Altham arrived in the summer of 1623 aboard the *Little James*, a pinnace of forty-four tons that James said was destined for use in fishing and fur-trading expeditions. Altham would stay in the New World for about a year, and "his devotion to the cause of colonization and taste for the heroic side of commerce rather than the ledger went beyond the ordinary, and helped keep English backing for the Pilgrim plantation alive when profit did not," added James.

In September 1623, Altham composed a letter to his eldest brother, Sir Edward, to assure Edward that all was well. He described Plymouth much the same way that

Pory had, "situated upon a high hill close unto the seaside, and very commodious for shipping."

The fishing off Plymouth in Cape Cod Bay was, Altham wrote, "beyond belief." Fog had forced a temporary halt at sea during one trip, but the weather eventually turned in their favor, and "in one hour we got 100 great cod." One fish, Altham insisted, "weighed 100 pound: it was as big a cod as ever was seen." Turbot was plentiful and one fish, he said, fed the entire crew. Sturgeon, salmon, bass, trout and eels, as Pory noted, were also abundant in Cape Cod Bay, as were clams and oysters. As rich as the fishing grounds in Cape Cod Bay were, the bay is more than a mere marine ecosystem. Its watershed lies beyond the sandy dunes, beaches and other microsystems. Where Pory gave only perfunctory notice, Altham swooned over the natural resources just ashore. "We have here as good timber as ever I saw-of many sorts…cedar, beech, pine, oak, and divers other sorts, of which we have here sent a sample of about two or three hundred pounds worth, and with it a good many beaver's skins and furs of divers sorts."

Ever the businessman and colonial wheeler and dealer, Altham promised to bring home "sarsaparilla and sassafras," which would sell well at the London market. Grapes, at least four different kinds, were plentiful, and plums and nuts were, too. The local Indians lived fourteen miles from Plymouth, called Patuxet by the Indians, "and their town is called Manomet." At one time in the not-too-distant past Altham reported, "likewise, in this bay wherein we live, in former time hath lived about 2000 Indians. Here is not one living now, nor not one living which belonged to this plantation before we came, so that the ground on which we are planted belongs to nobody."

Altham was a guest at the second marriage of Governor William Bradford, which the great Sachem Massasoit also attended, "where came with him his wife, the queen, although he hath five wives." Massasoit was accompanied by "four other kings and about six score men with their bows and arrows—where, when they came to our town, we saluted them with the shooting off of many muskets and training our men."

By all accounts, Altham thought well of Massasoit. "He is very subtle for a savage, and he goes like the rest of his men, all naked but only a black wolf skin he wears upon his shoulder." As a wedding gift to mark Governor Bradford's marriage to his second wife, Alice Southworth, a widow, Massasoit presented Bradford with "three or four bucks and a turkey." The feast also included "twelve pasty venisons…roasted venison and other such good cheer in such quantity that I could wish you some of our share," reported Altham.

Altham made mention in that 1623 letter to his brother of the troubles Massasoit had with a band of traders sent to present-day Weymouth by London merchant Thomas Weston through the Company of Adventurers for New Plymouth. There were sixty men, all without wives, who committed "notorious deeds" against Massasoit's people, including stealing corn. But Massasoit, clarified Altham, was a cautious man who "feared that when the English of Patuxet [Plymouth] did hear what they had done, then they would set upon the squaw sachem in the Massachusetts and so kill all the Indians in the Massachusetts."

Massasoit's initial plan was to murder all white colonists, including those at the settlement at Plymouth. But having been cured of an ailment by one of Bradford's men, Massasoit called off the plot and indeed warned Bradford of the coming carnage. "Whereupon the Governor, Mr. William Bradford (well worthy the place), sent Captain Standish with some six or seven others to the Massachusetts to bring away the head of him that made the broil."

Altham went back to England and then returned to the New World as a private citizen a few years later before returning to England sometime before July 1626. Apparently his goal of employment or other engagement with the colony did not come to pass. His elder brother, Sir Edward, saw to his future, and according to James, "He was sent to the Colony's fort at Surat and spent over two years in exploits around the Indian Ocean. The East India Company's business was a mixture of trade and raid—competing with the Portuguese for control of port cities in India and the trade to which they gave access." The high point for Altham included expeditions to Mozambique and Madagascar.

Altham died in January 1635 of an unknown cause.

Isaack de Rasierers

In his capacity as chief trading officer of the Dutch West India Company, the Holland-born Isaack de Rasierers (1595–1669 or later) traveled to Plymouth from Manhattan to meet with Governor William Bradford in October 1627. "He was the second-in-command to Pieter Minuit, and came to personally arrange to make a treaty with the Pilgrims for trade," said Hammond. De Rasierers traveled up from present-day New York aboard his barque *Nassau* and was met at the Aptucxet Trading Post, where Hammond says "they had to carry him in a litter across the isthmus, there, to Scusset River, a small marshy river navigable at high tide only, and from there took him up the coast to Plymouth." The author James wrote that de Rasierers had complained to Governor Bradford that the journey from Aptucxet to New Plymouth would require a lot of walking, something he had not done "so far this three or four years, wherefore I fear my feet will fail me."

His plan was to foster wampum as a currency among Indians who traded with the Dutch, which he did successfully. "Between de Rasierers' and Bradford's diaries, they mentioned the Dutch traded in linen cloth, Venetian glass beads, metal tools, sugar, and other staples," clarified Hammond.

In 1628, de Rasierers composed a letter to the merchant Samuel Blommaert, a director of the West India Company. He described the trading post at modern-day Bourne as "a house made of hewn oak planks, called Aptucxet, where they keep two men, winter and summer, in order to maintain the trade and possession. Here also they have built a shallop, in order to go and look after the trade in sewan, in Sloup's Bay [Narragansett Bay] and thereabouts."

Like Pory and Altham, de Rasierers's description of Cape Cod Bay is captivating:

> *New Plymouth lies in a large bay to the north of Cape Cod, or, Malabar* [Cape Cod, near Monomoy], *east and west from the said point of the cape, which can be easily seen in clear weather. Directly before the commenced town lies a sand-bank, about twenty paces broad, whereon the sea breaks violently with an easterly and east-northeasterly wind. On the north side there lies a small island where one must run close along, in order to come*

before the town; then the ships run behind that bank and lie in a very good roadstead. The bay is very full of fish, of cod, so that the Governor before named has told me that when the people have a desire for fish they send out two or three persons in a sloop, whom they remunerate for their trouble, and who bring them in three or four hours' time as much fish as the whole community require for a whole day—and they muster about fifty families.

The trading officer from Manhattan appeared impressed with Governor Bradford's colony.

New Plymouth lies on the slope of a hill stretching east towards the sea-coast, with a broad street about a cannon shot of 800 feet long, leading down the hill; with a [street] crossing in the middle, northwards to the rivulet and southwards to the land. The houses are constructed of clapboards, with gardens also enclosed behind and at the sides with clapboards, so that their houses and courtyards are arranged in very good order, with a stockade against sudden attack; and at the ends of the streets there are three wooden gates. In the center, on the cross street, stands the Governor's house.

After returning to Fort Amsterdam in Manhattan, de Rasierers came home to Holland. He married, raised a family and moved to Brazil to work for the West India Company.

With Colonial Progress, a Native Culture Is Slowly Dismantled

"Wee have given bargained and sold unto Mr William Bradford and Mr Thomas Prence and the Rest of the purchasers of Nausett these severall Tracts and are in hand payed by severall payments and in severall kinds: viz: in woulfe skines Indian Coates wampam kettles knives and the land sold and given to the purchasers of Eastham by Mattaquason." So reads the 1666 contract between the Wampanoag Sachem Mattaquason and the English settlers of Eastham and, later, Orleans, areas along Cape Cod Bay, after the two parishes split in 1797.

Though Nicholas Snow was an original founder of Eastham, when the southern parish was incorporated into Orleans in 1797, his farm sat on land once occupied by Sachem George. In fact, the streams, meadows, woodlands and coastlines upon which long-established Cape Cod clans like the Snows proudly draw their "native" status was for ten thousand years occupied by the Cape's original natives, the Wampanoag. Wherever the Plymouth Colony authorized settlements—all over modern-day southeastern Massachusetts—its land agents "bought" acreage from Indians, down to the last stone and sapling, according to a book on Indian deeds that the New England Historic Genealogical Society published in 2002. In June 1640, the land on which a former Indian territory called Cohannet was located was bought and renamed Taunton. To the west, Saughtuckquett was christened Duxborrow, or later Duxbury.

The Wampanoag believed that the land belonged to all who walked it, that its riches such as wood, game and fish could be shared and no one person or community could claim sole ownership. For many years they lived alongside the white settlers, sharing natural resources and forging relationships. In time it became clear that the English and Wampanoag viewed land ownership differently.

Land, upon which Henry Knowles kept an inn along the county road in Orleans in the nineteenth century, and where Simeon Higgins opened a stage and post office, was once called Nausett, farther south of Cape Cod Bay. Wampanoag men like Natnaught and Namanamock hunted rabbit and wild turkey in those parts, and no doubt fished in some of Orleans's sixteen freshwater ponds.

Jonathan Young's boot and shoe store that opened near Town Cove in Orleans in 1829 was most certainly in sight of where the hordes of Wampanoag men like Amaiwett Pumpmo or Namisco launched canoes made of either pine or chestnut. On land that evolved into Orleans, the Wampanoag culture was slowly suffocated in plain sight of its white neighbors, as the Indians' way of running their social order was now based on white law and ways. "The Indians of Potanumquut—now the south part of Orleans—had a court and magistracy of their own, established by the general court in 1682," wrote Simeon Deyo in 1890.

Disease and displacement took their toll and by 1800 few signs of living Wampanoag existed in Orleans. Two Indian cemeteries are in South Orleans, or were in 1890, Deyo wrote in *A History of Barnstable County*, including "on the land now owned by the heirs of William G. Nickerson, also at South Orleans."

Mattaquason, the sachem who literally signed away his lands in 1666 to Bradford & Company, never learned to read or write and was obviously illiterate—at least by English standards—when he signed away his ancestral lands. When he represented the Wampanoag at the sale of their lands, he signed off using the "marke," an inverted V, taught to him by the English.

Within decades the Indian culture would be dismantled, village by village. European diseases for which native people had no natural immunity would prove fatal. Most of the communities in islands north of Cape Cod Bay were now bare. "Most had been inhabited, but the same infection that had depopulated the Plymouth hillsides—formerly considered to have been smallpox, recently thought perhaps bubonic plague…had left these isles empty of cultivators," wrote Howard S. Russell in *Indian New England Before the Mayflower*.

Over the centuries, Native Americans had used their feet to weave slim but intricate pathways through dense bush and thick, virgin forests. "A fleet messenger might press a hundred miles over them in a single day," Russell explained. "Paths led across country from one river valley to another, between or over mountains, where usable streams were absent," making portage with birch bark canoes impossible. Today, many of these trails are covered by asphalt and are mainstream highways, streets and roads.

Even along the shores of Cape Cod Bay, Indian paths snaked along the watery corridor. At one time a dirt trail embraced Cape Cod Bay from what is today Provincetown to Plymouth. The sixty-mile path between Pawme—now Truro—and Plymouth, walked by three Pamet Indians in 1621 to announce the arrival of the *Fortune*, the first ship in the New World since the *Mayflower*, was well used even then.

That slim wisp of a dirt trail, says another legend, was used by Indians in 1627 to carry word from Nauset to Plymouth that the *Sparrow-Hawk* had wrecked in a storm on the Outer Cape. Once a twelve-inch-wide seventeenth-century footpath snaking into virgin forest teeming with bears and wolves, today the Old King's Highway (also known as Route 6A and Main Street) stretches thirty-four miles along the Cape's north side from Sandwich to Orleans and five towns in between, all along Cape Cod Bay. We can forgive one roadway having several names because that's what happens when a dirt path evolves over generations from a colonial dirt roadway into the nation's largest contiguous historic district.

If generations of oft-repeated assumptions are believed, after the native population waned, the former path served as a "major east-west thoroughfare for early settlers," reported the Cape Cod Commission. Later, "the narrow road became an extension of the Plymouth Colony's 'King's Highway' in the 17th century," a common generic British moniker given to many English-ruled roadways.

"Seldom broader than a cart's rutte," wrote one Englishman of the modest size of the path, adding, "the English sadly search up and down for a known way, the Indian paths being not above one foot broad, so that a man may travel many days and never find one."

Like street signs and historically appropriate informational markers that dot the Old King's Highway today, so too in yesteryear did the native people of Cape Cod mark their own roadways. "A slanting stick placed in the ground indicated that direction taken upon leaving the path, or an arrow marked in the dirt served the same purpose," wrote Leaman F. Hallett in "Indian Trails and their Importance to the Early Colonists." "The number in the party, the goods carried, the time and direction of departure and other information was available to friends who read the pre-arranged signs through messages emblazoned upon trees." Stones specially arranged on the ground were messages to fellow travelers. "No one was ever allowed to mar or deface its outline by using it for a camping ground," said Hallett.

If the beginnings of the Old King's Highway that rims Cape Cod Bay's underbelly were as humble as dirt, its function to link people to their neighbors to socialize, communicate with one another, trade, celebrate or fight was central to all portions of local history. "Over these early Indian trails there were constant migrations, seasonal removals from fishing to planting and hunting areas, and intertribal communication between villages along the way," said Hallett.

Eventually native tribes died off from disease and disenfranchisement as settlers claimed more Wampanoag land. Settlers used the path but slowly redefined its boundaries, widening it and cutting down trees along the way to accommodate horse-riding mailmen and stagecoaches. But never did the byway fall out of use. It merely supported each generation—native or colonist—that used it. So when Chief Mashantampaigne lay dying in the 1600s, his braves from the Nobscussett tribe—now contemporary Dennis—likely walked the pathway to pay him final homage near the same spot where Daniel Hall later built a homestead in 1723.

And the same spot in what is now Orleans where Stephen Snow settled in 1644 later proved an ideal location where fish were sun cured and salted. Up and down the north and south sides of the Old King's Highway, which embraces Sandwich, Barnstable, Yarmouth, Dennis, Brewster and Orleans, there's a story to be told at every turn, no matter what the century.

Unlike warm Midwesterners, New Englanders have a national reputation for frostiness, the roots of which were found in history. New Englanders had a policy of "warning out," or being disinvited from a community before setting down roots should they prove undesirable. Incorporated settlements along Cape Cod Bay were no exception. "In 1666, the Plymouth Colony, which by then included the Cape Cod towns of Sandwich, Barnstable, Yarmouth, and Eastham, passed a law that required the approval of the governor and two assistants before the right of inhabitancy could be granted," wrote historian Jim Coogan in *Cape Cod Companion*. "Some towns even went so far as to fine or censure inhabitants who received strangers into their homes." By 1700 the practice of "warning out" waned as core founding families left Cape Cod seeking larger plots of land in other parts of New England.

Shelter

English shelters along the shores of Cape Cod Bay from Plymouth south to Cape Cod were of European design. When Nicholas Snow and Edward Bangs stood in "uplands and meddows" in Nauset in 1644, they readied axe and saw to build a new township, later called Eastham. "The premise of colonization is that you have a housing shortage from day one," explained Tom Gerhardt, an interpretive artisan at Plimoth Plantation. The earliest Cape Cod homes were "very simple structures" said Gerhardt, one room only, though some had lofts "so it's hard to explain them as being one particular style."

Indeed, they were not the "low to the ground" domiciles that Thoreau described in the mid-nineteenth century. In 1644, immediate shelter equaled long-term survival, and our earliest settlers favored function and utility over proportion or beauty.

Archaeological excavations, written accounts and a knowledge of what Europeans were building 360 years ago have afforded historians the accuracy of early Cape townships strewn with small homes made of local hardwood, with cracks filled in with daub—a mixture of clay, loam and grass—pressed over lattice work. Lime, a prime ingredient for plaster, was rare to find on the Cape.

"In certain communities, if the carpenters came out of the east of England, the houses will follow that same pattern" wherever they were constructed in settlements sponsored by the Plymouth Colony. A one-room home took three months to build, and it wasn't unusual for walls to be three to four inches thick, hence a warm, snug shelter on freezing nights. Nearly every home had a chimney and most had lofts, especially homes constructed for large families.

A seven-foot-long pit saw helped to turn large trees into smaller timber or boards. Snow and Bangs brought with them different axes, too. Felling axes did just that, while a broad axe fashioned round trees into square beams. A lottery divided housing plots to avoid favoritism. The site of houses was left to an owner's discretion, and in no particular fashion. Land in Nauset challenged Pilgrim homebuilders. Historian Frederick Freeman called the area a "continuous pain, with now and then slightly rising grounds and corresponding depressions."

No formal zoning existed, except for clearly defined property lines, and where any usable land was. A settler's family might own land not adjoined to the main property where the house was. Lots were established by the size of a family, with each person in the household receiving half a rod by three rods, at 16.5 feet per rod.

Outhouses were unheard of in 1644. Chamber pots were the norm, with the contents dumped into the compost pile.

New Plymouth and Its People

When Thomas Paine of Truro, a rich landowner and judge, married Hannah Shaw of Plymouth in the late 1670s, it's anyone's guess how much the respected barrister or his new bride knew about sex. But clearly after saying "I do," they did. Between 1679 and 1705, Thomas and Hannah had fourteen children, with infants pouring from her fertile womb like the nearby "never-failing spring of pure water" said to run from a stream near their homestead. Women had as many children as their biology allowed.

Girls learned about sex from mothers and sisters, as did young men from their brothers, friends or fathers. Young folks too embarrassed to talk about human sexuality merely stumbled and fumbled their way through a minefield of hormones, petticoats and trousers. By some estimates, a third of young brides were pregnant when they married during the mid-eighteenth century and earlier.

Within seventeen years of its founding, New Plymouth expanded south to Cape Cod proper, establishing satellite communities in Sandwich in 1637 and Barnstable and Yarmouth in 1639. Independent and strong as these outposts were, the strict societal rules and religious regulations provided the framework of their lives.

"Occasionally people would get hauled into court for fornication before marriage" and charged five pounds for sexual relations before marriage, explained Carolyn Freeman Travers, research manager at Plimoth Plantation. "Providing a marriage happened, they were less upset."

In 1646, the general court ordered towns to keep marriage, birth and death registers. Rushed weddings—when a baby arrived six months after a ceremony, for example—were noted. "We further present Thomas Launders of the town of Sandwich, for having a child born within thirty weeks after marriage," read a court record from March 2, 1652. If a prison sentence of three days was ordered, "time in prison in early years of the colony meant being locked into a cage in which the prisoner was exposed to public view and abuse," wrote James and Patricia Deetz in *The Times of Their Lives: Life, Love, and Death in Plymouth Colony*. Hormones won out over the specter of public humiliation. "If you look in the 17th and 18th centuries in New England the church was powerful and in many ways was the civil authority," explained Jack Larkin, director of research, library and collections at Old Sturbridge Village. By the eighteenth century, Larkin explained, "no one is prosecuted any more for sexual violations except rape, for which there were only two reported cases in Plymouth County records and those cases weren't from the Cape.

The social policing of colonial sexual norms ran in cycles. Compared to Plimoth Colony, society loosened up around the time of the Revolutionary War, when an estimated 30 percent of all marriages occurred between a groom and a pregnant bride. Then, as the eighteenth century closed, girls weren't hovered over by a chaperone and couples were allowed to lie in bed, clothed, with their betrothed, separated by a bundling board—a swath of oak or pine—supposedly trading only endearments rather than sampling one another's bodies. Not surprisingly, many engaged couples found themselves expecting before their wedding. "Bundling disappears in the 19th century," clarified Larkin.

Interestingly, depending on the century, some sexual practices were regarded as worse than others. Masturbation began to appear in medical writings just before the middle of the nineteenth century. Larkin says young men believed self-gratification could lead to "nervous debility, depression and they'd lose their minds." Sodomy—homosexual behavior—was punishable by death in England, though in the Plymouth Colony every worker was valued so hanging someone reduced the workforce. Instead, those caught were whipped. "John Alexander & Thomas Roberts were both examined and found guilty of lewd behavior and unclean carriage one with another, by often spending their seed upon one another, which was proved both by witnesses & their own confession," wrote James and Patricia Deetz.

Life moved on along the shores of Cape Cod Bay. By 1680, the population in Plymouth was estimated at just fewer than 6,400. Four years later, the government of the Massachusetts Bay Colony dissolved. Barnstable County was incorporated on June 2, 1685, with the town of Barnstable as the shire town.

Captain Cyprian Southack

Cyprian Southack was a privateer hired by the government to salvage the wreck of the pirate ship *Whydah*, which wrecked off Nauset on the Cape's Outer Shore on April 26, 1717. The infamous Sam Bellamy was master. When his crew arrived, Cape Codders had already picked the wreck clean but left the pirate bodies for Southhack and his men to bury.

Amazingly, Captain Southack maneuvered a whaleboat from Nauset to Cape Cod Bay via a now-lost passage, which meant that in the early eighteenth century the Lower Cape was an island for a short time. Southack made a small mention of this:

The Place where I came
Through with a Whale Boat
Being ordered by ye Govern
To look after he Pirate Ship
Whido Bellame Command
Castaway he 26 of April 1717
Where I buried One Hundred
& Two Men Drowned

From historian David Kew's *Cape Cod History* website:

No one knows how long it took the Nauset tribe to dig out the first incarnation of the Cape Cod Canal with quahog-shell shovels, nor just when. It wasn't very hard to dig, since it was along the valley of the Boat Meadow River, the low land dividing what is now Eastham and Orleans, and the material to be removed was just sand and peat. This allowed the native whale-herders to safely move their pods from their sand-lance feeding grounds in Cape Cod Bay to their Limulus *"meadow" in Pleasant Bay via the canal, instead of the dangerous route north of Provincetown and through the Backside's shoals.*

Captain Southack died on Thursday, March 38, 1745, in Boston. He was eighty-four.

The first generations of white colonists mingled with native people, predominantly for work. One story has a Truro man, Joseph Swett, who according to his descendant, "drowned near his home in Truro 29 November 1716 with an Indian and four other Englishmen going from Eastham harbor to Billingsgate."

Shore Whaling

At a town meeting in 1680 in what is now Dennis, Samuel, John and Jeremiah Howes were appointed to "watch" for drift whales they could strip for oil, blubber and baleen. Legend points to Nantucket as the birthplace of whaling, but that's wrong; the industry began on Cape Cod Bay.

"While a number of explorers mentioned whales and the possibility of whaling, probably Captain John Smith (of Pocahontas fame) was the first with a whaling permit, and that was in 1614," declared Duncan Oliver, a former president of the Historical Society of Old Yarmouth and coauthor with the late Jack Braginton-Smith of *Cape Cod Shore Whaling—America's First Whalemen*. "The Pilgrims actually shot at one while anchored in Provincetown Harbor in 1620, and maybe that's the first attempt recorded by a colonist," added Oliver.

John Gorham of Cummaquid is recorded as one of the first off-shore whalers to use a boat based on design ideas of Jacobus Loper of Long Island, who visited Cape Cod Bay in 1680. Most likely Ichabod Paddock was there, and Paddock was the one who taught Nantucket residents the art of whaling.

The Wampanoag knew how to shore whale, cut up dead drift whales and fish from their off-shore shallops, but it was from colonists that they learned to whale well in open water.

"At some early but not certain date, land was appropriated and houses built to shelter the watchers in the seasons of winter and early spring when whales were most likely to be spotted," writes Nancy Thacher Reid in *History of Dennis*. Shore whaling continued even though deep-water whaling vessels were launched. Writing in 1840, Thomas Howes recounted that "should a whale be spotted in the Bay, it was all business for young and old. A large metal gong was struck repeatedly to summon all the men to come to the shore and assist in the capture of the leviathan."

Early whaleboats were very light, about twenty feet long and made of cedar lapstrake, said Oliver. "Four men rowed, along with a "harpooner" and a boat steerer (though he wasn't called captain), he added.

Given its size, relatively little of the whale itself was utilized in whaling's earliest days. The blubber was used for oil and the baleen for whalebone. The species of choice was the North Atlantic right whale, so named because it floated when dead, so it was the "right" leviathan to kill or harvest. It was a slow-moving species, it hugged the shoreline and its body contained a lot of whalebone and baleen. As right whales became scarce, other species like the fast-swimming finbacks came into vogue when in-shore whalemen took to boats as the fledging whaling industry evolved into deeper water. "They used a two-flued harpoon (they called them harping irons) to get 'fast' to the whale," said Oliver. "The harping iron was attached by a line to the boat or to a drogue which floated. When they got close to the whale, they used a lance and stuck it in the whale's vital areas to kill it."

In truth, Nantucket whalemen learned to shore whale from Ichabod Paddock of Yarmouth in the 1690s. Oliver says Nantucket whalemen started going out in small vessels, probably sloops, sometime around 1715.

CHAPTER FIVE

BOILING POINTS

*Our situation is truly delicate & critical. On the one hand we are in need of a strong federal
government founded on principles that will support the prosperity & union of the colonies. On the other
we have struggled for liberty & made costly sacrifices at her shrine and there are still many among us
who revere her name too much to relinquish (beyond a certain medium) the rights of man
for the dignity of government.*
—Mercy Otis Warren, Barnstable, September 29, 1787

During the American Revolution, colonial commercial traffic on Cape Cod Bay
and along the shore—from fishing to packet vessels to salt making—ground to
a halt when the British seized Provincetown. Simeon Deyo said, "The town has no
revolutionary history except the fact that it was a rendezvous for British men-of-war."
It is quite certain, however, that in 1782 the town was again inhabited, for a vote still
remains upon the records of the annual meeting of that year, appointing Seth Nickerson
Jr., Elijah N. Cook and Edward Cook a committee "to petition the general court for
liberty to obtain a protection from the British government for occupying the business of
fishing and bringing the effects into the adjacent states."

Cape Cod exported its sons to faraway battlegrounds, north into Boston, and other
points. A prominent family of the Revolution was the Otis clan of Barnstable. James Otis
Jr., a close associate of George Washington, delivered fiery arguments against the Writs
of Assistance belonging to George III. His brother, Joseph, also served under General
Washington. The youngest brother, Otis, clutched the Masonic Bible used to swear
Washington into office. The first secretary of the U.S. Senate, and first archivist, was
another brother, Samuel. Their sister, Mercy Otis Warren, was a Patriot who composed
plays, essays and poetry under her own name, the first woman in America to do so.

Much of the action during the American Revolution occurred on land next to Cape
Cod Bay, and not the bay itself. On a bitterly cold December night 235 years ago, John
Greenough of Wellfleet—a Harvard-educated schoolteacher—made an agreement that
would change his life. John had promised a distant cousin, Jonathan Clarke, a Boston tea
merchant, that he would sell two of the fifty-eight chests of East India tea salvaged from
the *William*, a brig owned by the Clarke family. The *William* was wrecked in a storm off
Provincetown, closer to the Outer shore than the bay, on December 10, 1773. Had the

vessel not been reduced to wooden shards in the nor'easter, it would have joined three other ships—the *Beaver*, *Dartmouth* and *Eleanor*—bound for Griffin's Wharf at Boston Harbor.

Jonathan Clarke was said to have traveled quickly to the Cape and caught up with Captain Joseph Loring of the *William*. Clarke and Loring arranged to have nearly all of the salvaged tea "placed on a lighter vessel" and taken to Boston "for safe keeping," according to an editor of the Greenough papers. Greenough was in Provincetown and in on the deal that Clarke struck with Captain Loring when he agreed to take the two chests of tea and sell them on the Cape.

In the meantime, back in Boston, one hundred men dressed as Mohawk Indians boarded three vessels on December 14, 1773. Many were Sons of Liberty who dumped $90,000 of English tea into Boston Harbor as thousands of colonists cheered from shore. The one million Americans who consumed tea bought theirs from colonial merchants who smuggled the tea past British tax collectors. The British had, in effect, "pre-taxed" the tea and then slashed its price to undercut the smugglers, enraging the colonists. Hence, the night of December 14, 1773, became the infamous Boston Tea Party, the uniquely American protest of the Tea Act passed by Parliament to help the British East India Company market its seventeen million pounds of unsold tea.

In 1773, the most efficient mode by which to spread news of British movements that threatened colonists' liberties was by a Committee of Correspondence. Samuel Adams, a cousin to John Adams, had established the first Committee in Boston. Soon nearly every town from Massachusetts to Georgia, including those on Cape Cod, had a Committee of Correspondence that kept alive the flames of colonial resistance.

Samuel Adams had heard that the *William* had wrecked off Provincetown, and pleaded with the Sandwich Committee of Correspondence to fight the possible unloading of tea at the Cape. Most of the tea, to the dismay of Adams and fierce Patriots, had arrived at a Boston safe house according to the arrangements Captain Loring had made with Jonathan Clarke, who worked with his father, Richard Clarke, a Boston tea merchantman. Greenough had been given two chests of tea by Jonathan Clarke when the latter was in Provincetown.

Quicker than you can say "smallpox," word crept from village to village that Schoolmaster Greenough of Wellfleet had British tea to sell, thanks to his relatives in Boston. For Greenough, assisting a relative to earn a few pounds proved a classic lesson in pre-Revolutionary politics in the Commonwealth.

From his home in Wellfleet, David Stoddard Greenough fired off a letter to his brother, Jonathan, who was still in Provincetown. David allegedly even hired a rider to get the note there fast, so worried was he for Jonathan's safety and that of his brother's family, not to mention the honor of the Greenough reputation.

"If you have bought any I'de advise you Rather to sink in the sea than to bring any of it here," wrote David Greenough. "I have been cautious of telling your wife the Threats I have heard many of them utter against you if you brought any of the Tea into this place." Clearly David Greenough feared the arrival of tainted tea in Wellfleet.

"The report that was brought here today by some credible Men to bring one or Two Chests of that Cursed Tea to Wellfleet to sell which is the cause of my hureing Gershon Rider to Cary this Letter to the cape to be left there for you." David Stoddard Greenough was incensed at his distant cousin, Jonathan Clarke, whom he blamed for dragging his brother, Jonathan Greenough, into the tea fray. "Clark (that tea devil) Lodg'd at your House Sunday night on his Return to Boston he told your wife of it which caus'd her great uneasiness she Desires of you not to bring one ounce here."

But, unfortunately, before Jonathan had received his brother's letter, Greenough had sold some tea to Colonel Willard Knowles of Eastham. Colonel Knowles, too, lived to regret the purchase. Colonel Knowles was called before the Eastham Committee of Correspondence, and in a letter begged Greenough to accompany him there. He implored, "Sir I Desier that you would be So good as to Come and advise with me about matters that we may Set our Caracters in a true Light." It's not known whether Greenough agreed to go.

For a time, Knowles lived under a veil of suspicion, even contempt, especially because the town stock of ammunition was lodged on his property, and he had purchased enemy tea. Because of that, a near riot erupted on March 7, 1774, and over eighty townsfolk unsuccessfully tried to "wrest the Towns Ammunition out of the Hands of Col. Knowles," wrote John Greenough to his father, Thomas. Only the arrival of the town militia calmed the crowd.

Feelings about the tea ran high. At an Eastham Town Meeting in spring 1774, the colonel was granted a communal pardon that in part read: "That Colo. Willard Knowles hath not forfeited the Confidence or good Esteem of this Town by buying & selling a small Quantity of Tea."

That March, Greenough composed a letter to Richard Clarke & Sons, a shipping agent for the East India Tea Company, explaining that his two chests of tea were now gone. He apologized for their loss and wrote, "I rely upon your honor whether I am to pay for that which is destroy'd or not." We don't know how the Clarkes responded, nor from copies of the existing letters and documents on the tea case do we know exactly how the tea was disposed of.

John Greenough was summoned before the Wellfleet Committee of Correspondence in April 1774. In his defense, Greenough denounced the tax on tea, but decried the destruction of what was the private property of the East India Company, the facts of which will apparently remain elusive. "Nor do I think any of them would refuse the India Company's Tea if it had not been subjected to this Duty now laid on it," he asserted.

When all was said and done, for his trouble, a disgraced Greenough lost his prestigious post as schoolteacher in 1774, and for a time his father, brother and other family members were none too happy with him. Eventually, Greenough moved back into the good graces of his family and community. Greenough was appointed to the Wellfleet Committee of Correspondence and Safety in 1778 and briefly served in the militia. A year later, the former schoolteacher was appointed by the Massachusetts Board of War as "Superintendent for saving the Stores" of the British *Somerset* when the sixty-four-gun man-of-war wrecked off Peaked Hill Bars Truro in November 1778. Clearly Greenough had regained a measure of respect in what his brother would later call "the Cursed Tea Affair."

We know little about Greenough after the infamous tea incident. He left Wellfleet and moved his clan to Boston, where he died in 1781.

The Wreck of the *General Arnold*

Barnabas Downs was born in Barnstable, the county seat, in October 1757, and labored as a farmer before joining American forces battling the English for independence. Working as a privateer, Downs was aboard the brigantine *General Arnold* under Captain James Magee; the ship carried twenty guns and a crew complement of 120. On Thursday, December 24, 1778, the *General Arnold* was underway from Nantasket bound for the West Indies alongside another privateer, the *Revenge*, which was commanded by General Ezekiel Burroughs. The *Revenge*, a smaller vessel at only ten guns, slipped through a severe storm but the *General Arnold* was not as lucky. Nearly a dozen Cape Cod boys and men were aboard, including Cornelius Merchant, age fifteen. A wicked nor'easter trapped the *General Arnold* in Cape Cod Bay off Plymouth Harbor.

"Capt. Magee was a good sailor," wrote Amos Otis in *The Genealogical Notes of Barnstable Families*. "The sixteen main deck guns were lowered into the hold, the topmasts were struck, the sails snugly furled, long scopes given to the cables…all these precautions did not prevent her from dragging her anchors. She drove towards the shore and struck on White Flat, a shoal in Plymouth Harbor."

With no shelter below and water ankle deep, the crew was in trouble. Heavy snow began to fall. By late Saturday, with the tide receding, at least the freezing spray no longer showered the crew. Come Sunday morning, with winds out of the northwest, the cold increased. By now, thirty sailors had died, having slowly frozen to death. High winds had washed a few overboard, only to drown. Three crewmen took a yawl for help but they never returned.

"Until now we had hopes of escape, but just before night we looked into the hold and saw the casks floating about; this drove us to despair, and we fortook the pumps without a ray of hope…Many of the people began to pray, and I went into the cabin and sat upon one of the gun-carriages," Downs remembered. "Death appeared inevitable, and we waited every moment for its approach!"

All this time the horrified citizens of Plymouth watched, helpless, unable to navigate the ice-ridden bay to assist the crew of the *General Arnold*.

Finally the storm died on Sunday, December 27, but the severe cold remained. "We saw Plymouth and a number of people coming along the shore for our relief: we could discern them push off two boats and make an hard trial to come to us, but the harbour was so full of ice they could not reach us." Downs said he then laid down on the quarter-deck until Monday.

Rescue arrived on Monday with only thirty-two men still alive, but barely. "When they were looking around to collect the survivors, they at first supposed me to be dead, but feeling one of my eye-lids move they took me up and laying me in the board carried me ashore," Downs recounted. He was taken to a tavern, where his frozen clothing was cut away. "I was then placed in a bed and having my teeth forced open had some cordials poured down my throat, but I have no remembrance of any of these transactions."

The bodies of seventy-two dead crewmen were recovered and laid in Mill River to thaw and then placed in coffins. Plymouth held a community funeral. "So solemn and affecting a spectacle is rarely witnessed…Their friends were far away; yet real mourners were there, the people of old Plymouth attended in droves. The profound solemnity of the scene choked the utterance of the officiating clergyman," according to Amos Otis. Barnabas Lothrop survived initially but later succumbed onshore.

The dead crewmen included familiar Barnstable names: Captain James Russell, a militia leader; Thomas Carsley; and, according to Downs, "a negro," Boston Crocker, a servant to Joseph Crocker.

Downs recovered but his feet were amputated. In later years he used crutches or walked on his knees. Downs was married in 1784 and sired five children—the eldest named for Captain James Magee. He died in 1817.

Not every Cape Codder born along the bay in the eighteenth century stayed put. Though some took to the land and others to the sea, musket and war making and long bouts of travel were preferable to the plow or fishing pole.

Indeed, by our standards, families were large. Having ten or more children was not uncommon and farmers were hard pressed to provide prime acreage for all their sons, so some looked off-Cape for work. "By the 1730s and 1740s, the Cape and Barnstable area was the poorest part of Massachusetts, with most of the little available land taken," according to John Grenier in *The First Way of War, American War Making on the Frontier*.

"In the summer of 1744," Grenier wrote, John Gorham of Barnstable, Massachusetts—great-grandson of John Gorham I of King Philip's War and grandson of John Gorham II of Benjamin Church's rangers of King Philip's and King William's Wars, and heir to a family tradition that was now seven decades old of participating in New England's wars—began recruiting men for one of the Nova Scotian companies of rangers. Though the war didn't touch Cape Cod, a Cape Codder immersed himself in warfare elsewhere.

Salty Inventions and Tensions

In 1776, John Sears, a fisherman, and his wife, Deborah Crowell Sears, lived in Yarmouth's eastern parish, Quivet Neck, which became East Dennis when the town of Dennis was incorporated in 1793. They raised a family of nine children along the shores of Cape Cod Bay. That year, John invented a new industry: salt making.

Nancy Thacher Reid, author of *Dennis, Cape Cod*, said Sears built a shallow wooden vat up off the ground by a few feet, filled it with sea water and waited. Between some ups and downs, he ended the first season's try with eight bushels of "fine white salt." Caulking his vat the following year to stop leaking produced thirty bushels. Though not quite a success just yet, John endured his neighbors' taunts of "Sears Folly." Two years later, though, a bilge pump rumored to have been from the wreck of the HMS *Somerset* off Nauset was adapted to Sears's vat. Reid wrote, "Once it was seen that Sleepy John had a workable scheme, the ideas began to roll. In future years Hattil Kelley and Reuben Sears would come up with a method by which the vats could be covered quickly in inclement weather. Another friend suggested that a windmill be rigged to work the pump."

As an industry, salt making took off and soon Cape Cod Bay's coastlines were dotted with vats. Within decades, salt would become a tool by which the British extorted money from Cape Codders living on or near Cape Cod Bay.

Ubiquitous wooden salt vats dotted the shoreline of Cape Cod Bay. *Courtesy of Stanley and Bonnie Snow, Orleans.*

Simeon L. Deyo wrote in his 1890 *History of Barnstable County, Massachusetts,*

> *The great scarcity of corn which prevailed upon the Cape during the war compelled some of the more daring captains to run the risk of being taken by the enemy, and by discreet and crafty maneuvering they would succeed in bringing a load now and then from the southern ports, and necessarily it was sold at very high prices.*

Matthew Mayo pointed two pistols at British marines aboard an English schooner in Cape Cod Bay in 1814, threatening to shoot anyone who came close. Depending on which account you believe, he then succeeded in single-handedly capturing the British warship and its crew, reversing the role thrust upon him as a prisoner of the British, who had caught him smuggling goods through the blockade that clamped down tightly on Cape Cod during the War of 1812.

The British made Captain Mayo pilot their schooner through Cape Cod Bay as they searched for privateers who penetrated their naval blockade. When a sudden gale distracted the British, Mayo snuck below, stole two guns from an officer's cabin and hatched an escape plan. "We have it on indisputable authority that this valiant son of Eastham, singlehandedly, captured a British vessel of war with its entire crew, and it is doubtful if in the whole history of our sea fights this gallant deed of individual daring has ever been surpassed," wrote Michael Fitzgerald a century ago.

The War of 1812 cut off trade supplies to Cape Cod. Rather than let their families go without necessities like flour, sugar, molasses and cloth, many hometown captains traded their prestigious top hats for the caps of privateers, sneaking grounded fishing schooners and whaleboats to Boston and New York for goods and food otherwise not grown or manufactured here. "With the Cape, it was small investments and quick returns, or nothing," wrote Henry Kittredge in *Cape Cod: Its People and Their History.* "Since this was precisely the sort of trade that the Government could most effectively stop, it is no wonder that the hostility to the Embargo blazed even hotter on the Cape than in the larger seaports."

Along with Mayo on that ill-fated smuggling trip was another Eastham captain, Winslow Knowles. The British told Knowles to sail back to Boston and come up with another $300 in ransom money. Mayo and Knowles, and their confiscated provisions, were first taken aboard a schooner apparently commandeered by the British for local patrols. When Knowles was let go, Mayo was held on the HMS *Spencer*, the British flagship for Cape waters, and eventually transferred back to the schooner as a pilot. Then the gale hit, and onboard with Mayo were three British officers and twenty men, all well armed with cutlasses, pistols and muskets. As the schooner's pilot, during the storm "Captain Mayo advised them to make a harbor under Billingsgate Point; but it being his intention to deceive the enemy, and, if possible, to recapture the vessel and make prisoners of all on board, he anchored in bad holding ground," wrote Enoch Pratt in his 1844 *History of Eastham.*

"The gale still continuing, he went forward unobserved, and with his penknife partly severed the cable, which soon parted. He then advised the officers to make a harbor to the leeward, about ten miles distant," added Pratt. Before long the schooner had grounded "on the flats of Eastham," but Mayo allegedly told the wary British they had only hit a bar far offshore. To pass the time, he offered to crack open a barrel of rum below deck, which was confiscated when he and Captain Knowles were captured, according to an account by Jeremiah Digges in *The Cape Cod Pilot*. Pratt claims, "He gave them a gimblet, with which they tapped a cask of West India rum, and drank till they were intoxicated."

Mayo allegedly locked most of the crew in below and stole pistols. Once the tide ebbed and their schooner was grounded, the British realized they'd been duped, but, allegedly drunk and locked away, most of them could do nothing. Digges's account states that Captain Mayo heaved "the rest of the ship's arms overboard, battened down the hatch on twenty-one sailors in the fo'cs'le, took over the helm and gunpoint, and steered the schooner for home" and then grounded it on the flats. Pratt's account was equally dramatic: "Captain Mayo immediately threw overboard the arms that were on deck, drew out his pistols and threatened to shoot anyone who should attempt his life."

No doubt the truth lies somewhere in the middle. The local militia—alerted that a schooner of unknown origin had stranded on the flats—took over and marched the captured British to Thomas Crosby's tavern, where "they were put under guard for the night" and then set free the next day; why the prisoners weren't kept in custody isn't known.

Isolation from major sources of trade during wartime made Cape Cod unique in its need to smuggle food and supplies while its economy, ships and smaller vessels lay rotting at dock. Ship owners in Boston and Salem fared better; their captains stayed overseas and continued to trade, eventually returning after the war with gold in their strongholds. Cape Codders' counterparts from larger seaports like Baltimore and New York raided English ships largely for profit and revenge. Cape Codders ran smuggling runs south, too, toward New York. Captains Mayo and Knowles were just two of these smugglers who by all accounts stuck to the bayside Boston run.

A more obvious question could be raised regarding how the British provisioned their own vessels that patrolled Cape Cod Bay and the Outer Cape, since they couldn't rely on confiscated goods to provide food and drink for all their marines. "I would be very surprised if many were not also supplying the British fleet," said Robert Allison, PhD, a Provincetown summer resident and professor of history at Suffolk University. "It would be impossible for the British to maintain the blockade without fresh provisions. Were the locals supplying the British?"

Battle of Orleans

The War of 1812 is one of those "easily forgotten" conflicts in which the United States fought. The United States declared war on Great Britain on June 12, 1812, over British impressments of American soldiers in the English war against France. Disputes over the Northwest Territories added to the boiling pot of issues, along with the British blockade against France, which interrupted commercial trade in America.

The so-called Battle of Orleans wasn't really a battle, more like a little skirmish, but it adds to the patina of civic pride despite being absent from the rolls of historic battles recorded for the War of 1812. On December 12, 1814, the HMS *Newcastle* had run aground in the darkness off the southern tip of Billingsgate Shoal in Cape Cod Bay. The grounding occurred while the *Newcastle* was en route from Boston to Provincetown, headquarters to English warships in charge of patrolling Cape Cod waters.

That day, Captain Lord George Stuart ordered spare rigging and spars tossed overboard to lighten the load as he and his men tried to refloat the *Newcastle*. It is assumed that an incoming tide ferried the cargo toward shore, where locals dragged the rigging onto land. "There they fell on the tackle with axes and hatchets in an effort to reduce it to useless debris in case the enemy made a recovery attempt," wrote scholar Richard K. Murdoch in July 1964 for the quarterly journal *The American Neptune*.

The *Newcastle* freed itself the next day, and from December 13 up until the morning of December 19, Captain Stuart was apparently fixated on finding the spare rigging. Captain Stuart ordered his crew to search for the missing tackle on a yawl boat. Underway, the yawl was said to give chase to a Yankee sloop, the *Camel*, bound for Orleans with badly needed provisions. The *Camel* ran aground near Rock Harbor Creek and all but one Yankee crewman fled. A quick exam of the tangled tackle was made. Only the smaller spars could be saved. Then, British marines took the lone crewman aboard the yawl to help navigate the small vessel toward Provincetown to meet up with the *Newcastle*, which lay in anchor off Truro.

The American purposely ran the vessel aground, in fact not far from his home at Wellfleet. Fed up with poor shipboard conditions, and seizing this opportunity to escape, the five British seamen deserted, walked through shallow water toward shore in Wellfleet and were taken into custody by the militia and transported under guard to Boston.

By the morning of December 18, 1814, Captain Stuart learned that folks in Orleans had "taken possession of the remaining spars," according to Murdoch, and "that there were a number of small American vessels at anchor in Rock Harbor Creek, long known as a haven for coastal boats trying to penetrate the blockade of Boston." A plan was made to step onto American soil the next morning.

Murdoch continued,

> In the meantime, the inhabitants of Wellfleet had taken possession of the abandoned yawl and had unloaded some of the provisions that had originally been taken from Camel. The spars and sails were too cumbersome to remove far from the water's edge. To ascertain the exact fate of the yawl and its crew on the morning of 14 December, Captain Stuart, then at anchor in Cape Cod Bay off Truro, dispatched a small recently captured fishing boat in the general direction of the Orleans-Eastham shore. After scouting along the coast as far as the southern end of Billingsgate Island the boat returned to Newcastle with information that the yawl lay abandoned and it appeared that its cargo was on shore in the hands of the inhabitants. An armed barge was then dispatched to recover the yawl and apparently this mission was accomplished on the eighteenth without opposition from the townspeople lined up along the shore.

On the morning of December 16, Captain Stuart learned there was a small contingent of Yankee vessels at Rock Harbor Creek. This area was a known loading and off-loading area for privateers skirting the blockade.

On the morning of December 19, Captain Stuart ordered four armed barges from *Newcastle* to look into whether that spare tackle could be reused. Leading the way aboard one of the barges was Lieutenant Frederick Marryat, a midshipman, Charles Underwood and twenty-two sailors and marines. Lieutenant Marryat ordered the other three barges to hold the mouth of the creek. The British found the sloop *Camel* up the estuary, along with two other sloops, *Washington* and *Nancy*, and the schooner *Betsy*, whose cargo hold carried salt.

"Although none of the crew of the four American vessels were on board when the enemy barge entered the creek, there at work at the nearby salt works several men who witnessed the British landing and the seizure of the four vessels," reported Murdoch. All Yankees fled except one who was held prisoner while the alarm sounded to the townsfolk of Orleans. The British, led by Midshipman Underwood, commandeered the *Betsy* and made ready to sail her to *Newcastle*. Instead of going east, though, the hostage pilot sailed west, in growing darkness and "thick snow squalls," as Murdoch noted, and ended up in Yarmouth, in the ready hands of the militia there.

In the meantime, Marryat, still at Rock Harbor Creek, exchanged musket shots with several Orleans militiamen at select positions along Cape Cod Bay on routine sentinel duty. The English marines returned fire. Here's where various stories stray from one another. One British marine was reported killed there, but no locals were wounded or killed. The British retreated. And that simple exchange of gunpowder was the extent of the Great Battle of Orleans.

During the War of 1812, the British fought the Americans at ten United States sites, mostly in the Great Lakes area. The only New England skirmish was along the shores of Lake Champlain in Vermont. Though the war did not extend into Massachusetts much beyond several skirmishes on Cape Cod, New England was affected through its industries and a virtual paralysis of its merchant fleets until the Treaty of Ghent was signed on December 24, 1814, and ratified by the United States in February 1815.

It took the government nearly sixty years to reward the homegrown soldiers who fought in the Battle of Orleans. On March 3, 1855, Congress passed land warrants of 160 acres and a few pensions to sailors or soldiers who had fought in any skirmish during the War of 1812. It's not known if any veterans in Orleans put in for that land bounty. But we do know that Captain Stuart, after learning what had transpired with the Yankee militia, referred to the soldiers as "those wretches in Orleans."

> *I call upon you to come forward with a contribution of One Thousand Dollars for the preservation of your salt works which as I consider of Public Utility will otherwise be destroyed.*
> —*Richard Ragget, Commodore, HMS* Spencer

The British-American conflict over salt was not settled on a ruddy earthen field in Lexington, but the marine landscape of Cape Cod Bay during the War of 1812. The

Cape Cod Bay in 1795. *Courtesy of the William Brewster Nickerson Memorial Room, Cape Cod Community College.*

English commodore of the HMS *Spencer* extorted money from Cape Cod Bay towns in exchange for sparing each community's saltworks. Brewster was no exception.

According to Ragget, $4,000 would be the necessary "contribution to guarantee" that Brewster's saltworks would not be destroyed. This "contribution" secured the British hold on the Cape's economy during the English blockade. Vessels belonging to local captains—owned by either fishermen or merchants—rotted with few incoming supplies of food and daily necessities. Until the war was over, Cape Codders lived on what they could grow locally or smuggle in. Ragget's "contribution" was brutally wise, because salt was to Brewster what fishing was to the Cape's economy in those early decades of the nineteenth century: nothing short of its lifeblood.

Salt preserved large quantities of fish, meaning that people could eat off the sea long after the nets were hauled in. In 1837, one of the earliest years for which "harvest" information was available, sixty saltworks operating in Brewster yielded 27,400 bushels alone. After reading Ragget's letter, nervous selectmen called a meeting for ten o'clock Sunday morning, September 18, at the Brewster Meetinghouse "on the very sudden and urgent occasion that had arisen," according to town meeting records.

Elijah Cobb was picked to moderate and Reverend Simpkins led the assembly in prayer. Within minutes, an action plan was set in motion. Five Brewster men would leave town immediately to connect with neighboring villages and spread the word about Ragget's extortion threat. Cobb hauled off to Orleans and Eastham, Solomon Freeman rode into Chatham and Captain Benjamin Berry took flight to Harwich, from which Brewster had seceded in 1803. Off to Dennis flew Captain Thomas Seabury. "Mr. Kenelm Winslow and Capt. Freeman Foster, to Yarmouth and Barnstable," wrote Frederick Freeman in *The History of Cape Cod* in 1862.

Delegates from each town would be asked to Brewster's meetinghouse at six o'clock that evening to compare notes and decide what to do. Brewster took no chances and folks hardly stood idle. Wrote Freeman, "The commander of Artillery in Brewster engaged horses to be in readiness for the ordnance; and that a committee, one from each school-district, ascertain promptly how many over 45 years of age and under 60, including others exempt, may be found who will join the artillery, as there is a deficiency in said company."

Late that afternoon, Soloman Freeman and the other messengers reported back from Brewster's neighbors and the news wasn't good: "that the town of Brewster can make no dependence on any of our neighbors for assistance in our alarming and distressed situation." Isolated by its municipal peers, Brewster caved and the selectmen came up with what they thought was the only solution.

Commodore Ragget, it would appear, had Brewster by the cannonballs. "After much consultation and deliberation, it was voted that the com. of safety who went on board his B.M. Ship *Spencer*, go again this night and make the best terms possible with Com. Ragget as respects the $4,000 demanded; and that said committee be, and are, clothed with sufficient power from this town, to make such terms."

But that didn't sit well with the municipal rank and file, either, and the attendees at the town meeting came up with a second option that seemed more palatable. Freeman wrote, "It was then 'voted to choose a com. of disinterested persons from out of town, to say what kind of property shall be taxed for the contribution-money, if any must be paid; said com. not to be owners of salt-works, and to be chosen at some future day.'"

When committee members boarded the *Spencer* to bargain for lower terms, Commodore Ragget wouldn't budge. "They used their best endeavors to obtain a relinquishment of a part of the sum demanded, but could not obtain the abatement of a dollar." Town meeting members then voted to pay up by October 1. Only two people, Theodore Berry and Joseph Snow, voted against the grain.

Brewster quickly raised $4,000 by taxing nearly everything in sight, according to Frederick Freeman: "The salt-works, buildings of every description, and vessels owned in this town of every description frequenting, or lying on, the shores." No one living in Harwich, from which Brewster split in 1803, was taxed. The cash was delivered to Ragget on September 30, 1814, a day before Ragget's deadline.

"That the Inhabitants and Proprietors of the Salt Works at Brewster have come forward with a contribution to prevent the destruction of their salt-works and town; And I do hereby acknowledge to have received the same as a contribution; And I do also guarantee the safety of the said salt-works and town at Brewster during the present War," wrote Ragget.

Eastham was the only other town that paid Commodore Ragget any money, a sum of $1,000. The other towns flat refused. In May 1815, Brewster appealed to the state legislature for reimbursement for the "contribution" of $4,000. "It is understood that no relief was obtained," wrote Freeman. Up until a few years ago, the 1814 extortion still had not died out in Brewster. During the country's bicentennial year in 1976, a group of Brewsterites wrote Queen Elizabeth II asking for a refund, with interest. Her Majesty declined.

In September 1816, a nor'easter hit Buzzards Bay and Cape Cod Bay, uprooting trees, "buildings prostrated; salt-works destroyed; vessels scattered from their moorings, and driven ashore," recounted one eyewitness. A beautiful, calm bay can turn into a disaster area on a weather dime when storms strike.

CHAPTER SIX

INDUSTRY AND FAMILY

Now we saw countless sails of mackerel fishers aboard on the deep, one fleet in the north just pouring round the Cape, another standing down toward Chatham, and our host's son went off to join some lagging member of the first which had not yet left the Bay.
—Henry David Thoreau

Fisheries

The nation's first sustainable fishery took hold in Cape Cod Bay in the seventeenth century. The fishery was not formally structured as it is by government regulations today; it didn't need to be. Fish stocks were plentiful, and merely by casting a net overboard, the harvesting of cod, herring, eel and other species was practically effortless.

As an industry, fishing escalated in the seventeenth century but abruptly halted to a near-end during the Revolutionary War. Out of sheer necessity, farming continued during the war years in communities lining Cape Cod Bay. Gristmills were in continual use in communities along Cape Cod Bay. "Within a few years of the *Mayflower* mills were built at Plymouth and then, to save long and laborious journeys, at Sandwich," wrote Albert Perry Brigham. "Surface streams with suitable fall are so rare on the Cape that wind power was invoked, and the windmill became a common object in the landscape."

Men in the Old Colony frittered away free hours scouring Cape Cod Bay for dead whales. "To watch for drift whales was a distinct part of public duty in Plymouth," insisted Brigham, "and various towns record regulations to secure private and town rights in such spoils. Boats were launched for whaling and a new enterprise was born. An official letter to England in 1688 asserted the great profit of whale killing to the Plymouth colony…As early as 1737, Provincetown was sending a dozen whalers to Davis Strait in the far north," Brigham explained, and "at the opening of the Revolution, Wellfleet, Barnstable, and Falmouth had thirty-six whaling vessels, mostly in northern waters."

Maritime muscle equaled political clout. As the eighteenth century drew to a close, Old Colony communities had hundreds of vessels on the water—more than a thousand ships—with a land-based infrastructure to support and maintain various fleets. Brigham

A small crowd around a dead finback whale in Provincetown. *Courtesy of the William Brewster Nickerson Memorial Room, Cape Cod Community College.*

said Plymouth alone had sixty vessels. The English-based Old Colony was in turn responsible for dominating the French in North America.

Fishing escalated after the Revolutionary War. One yarn Brigham brought to life in his 1920 report: "A picture of the industrial ruin the war brought to the Cape is drawn in the plea of Fisher Ames in 1789, explaining why, if fishing was so decayed and profitless, the men did not leave the region. He said, and it was no uncommon mark in those days, 'they are too poor to live there and are too poor to remove.'"

The fisheries recovered following the Revolutionary War. By 1850, stocks of codfish fell but mackerel rose. Wellfleet's mackerel fleet numbered seventy-five schooners "as late as 1860," according to one source, with the trade beginning there in 1826. The same was true for the fishing communities along Cape Cod Bay in Yarmouth, Dennis and on the south side, Chatham and Harwich. In time, small fleets left Provincetown for the Labrador Coast—though most fishermen worked in sight of shore there—and to the Grand Banks, and these sons of Provincetown were gone for weeks at a time. Day fishermen lived mostly on the south side of Cape Cod, working Nantucket Sound from towns such as Harwich, and to the north, in Rock Harbor in Orleans. In later generations, the majority of the Cape Cod Bay fishing fleet hailed from Provincetown. While these later generations might have dropped line off Georges Bank, Grand Banks or any points on the compass, they often transited Cape Cod Bay.

On many a cold morning in 1816, between midnight and dawn, nine-year-old Nathaniel Ellis Atwood of Provincetown was awakened by his father and put to work on a fishing boat, and once the sun rose his breath hung in the frigid air like the steam rolling off the rim of a hot bowl of soup. Like many of his peers, Nathaniel worked all day, then turned in, until his father's gentle touch would again claim his sleep. Even when grown,

Cape Cod in 1838. *Courtesy of the William Brewster Nickerson Memorial Room, Cape Cod Community College.*

Nathaniel would know no life other than fishing, which fueled the economy of the sandy fist of Cape Cod and put Provincetown on the map as a leading port.

For the next ninety years, Cape Codders and their Yankee counterparts had New England waters to themselves, until three distinct foreign groups arrived. From Boston came the Irish who, according to Captain Atwood, introduced beam trawl fishing to Provincetown in the 1860s. Next were the Portuguese, who were attracted to the Cape because of whaling and decided to settle here. Several decades after arriving behind the Irish in the 1860s, the Portuguese, declared Historian George Bryant of Provincetown, invented the technique of dragging for fish around 1895. Signing on to join fishing crews were the Scottish Gaels from Cape Breton.

Young Nathaniel, who learned the fishing trade from his father, kept his hand in fishing his entire life. As a young man, Captain Atwood was a successful skipper who survived two shipwrecks within two weeks of one another in 1851. After returning to shore, he served as a selectman, state representative and customs collector for the port of Provincetown. He was recognized as a respected ichthyologist. He died in 1886 at the age of seventy-nine, though his career dovetailed with Provincetown's glorious fishing days.

A small fleet of quahaug boats at Rock Harbor, Orleans. *Courtesy of Stanley and Bonnie Snow, Orleans.*

Weir fishermen. *Courtesy of Stanley and Bonnie Snow, Orleans.*

Sweeping view of Provincetown Harbor. *Courtesy of the Historical Society of Old Yarmouth.*

The 1860s were the best years for salt cod fishing—the premier sort of fishing—in Provincetown. In 1866, according to Bryant, ninety-one vessels from Provincetown were engaged in salt cod fishing: nineteen used trawls in the Gulf of St. Lawrence, with seventy-two more on the Grand Banks. "This fleet brought back 93,663 quintals of fish and used 4,098 barrels of salt clams in catching them," wrote Bryant in a 1976 paper. (A quintal, Bryant says, is "100 weight," or about 100 pounds.)

Writing about Provincetown's fishing history is challenging because the industry was complex, despite the simplistic nature of eighteenth- and nineteenth-century culture in an unsophisticated backwater sand lot that was the Lower Cape then. Being situated in the far eastern lap of Cape Cod Bay provided a keen geographic vantage point for generations of Provincetown fishing families to strike out in any direction, even into the bay itself.

Mackerel, which traveled in schools as far south as North Carolina, were packed in barrels in water and salt; think "pickled." Once onshore, crews would salt and pack the fish in barrels. Cod, as Bryant noted, were a groundfish, or "bottom fish," and were hauled up and salted below deck and then piled "like firewood" with salt between them. Even choosing the right bait was a delicate process. Pickled clams and mussels from Provincetown provided immediate bait so crews could get to work straightaway. As a last resort if fish weren't available, local sea birds were caught and chopped up for bait.

Lining Provincetown's waterfront were dozens of wharves, large and small, on which tons of cod, mackerel, whiting and other species were dried, salted and flaked and then packaged for shipping off-Cape, decade after decade. Fish was sold salted, pickled and, later, delivered fresh and shipped in ice to Boston or New York City. Much of it was shipped by rail once the Old Colony Line reached Provincetown in July 1873. In the 1890s, a cannery opened in the East End behind the old Consolidated Cold Storage Company, one of many local firms that depended on steam engines to keep their ocean produce frozen and ready for shipment.

A scene of Provincetown from Old Town Hall. *Courtesy of the William Brewster Nickerson Memorial Room, Cape Cod Community College.*

Icebergs off Long Point, Provincetown. *Courtesy of the William Brewster Nickerson Memorial Room, Cape Cod Community College.*

"There was nothing else," declared Bryant. "There was no farming," he reasoned, "everyone was connected to fishing." So intertwined were Provincetown and its fishing that it can be well argued that fishing—or one of its related industries such as salt making, sail making or salt making, to name a few—bought and paid for the brick and lumber for buildings, cloth for clothing and the very food on any supper table in any home in Provincetown during most of the nineteenth century. Often men fished on Georges Bank. "By 1866, some seventy-two of Provincetown's ninety-one salt cod fishing vessels were

A wintry landscape in Provincetown Harbor. *Courtesy of the William Brewster Nickerson Memorial Room, Cape Cod Community College.*

Steamboat Wharf in Provincetown Harbor was a major wharf in town, one of dozens before the notorious Portland Gale of 1898 destroyed all but a handful. *Courtesy of the William Brewster Nickerson Memorial Room, Cape Cod Community College.*

Bankers. They brought back a huge harvest in that good and lucky year, 10.5 million pounds of fish (93,663 quintals), using up in the process 4,098 barrels of salt clam bait," wrote Russell Bourne in *The View From Front Street: Travels Through New England's Historic Fishing Communities.*

As the nineteenth century drew to a close, so did the fishing heyday of Provincetown, whose sole grip on the enterprise waned as other ports gained prominence.

Shipbuilding and Packet Lines on Cape Cod Bay

If fishing saw its glory days in the nineteenth century, the same can be said for the construction of wooden boats. We don't think of Cape Cod Bay as a haven for shipbuilding, mostly because its harbors weren't deep enough to support vast wooden hulls, but smaller ships were constructed along its shores. "During the 18th century, Cape Cod men turned ever more seaward, carrying produce, such as onions, corn and flax to Boston in their own vessels," wrote Haynes Mahoney in *Yarmouth's Proud Packets.* "Soon they built sturdy little schooners capable of coastal trading which brought them as far as the Caribbean, exchanging salt cod for rum."

Packets—water taxis used to transport people and trade goods—flitted about Cape Cod Bay like greenhead flies off the Great Marsh in July, whizzing back and forth between Boston and Plymouth, and back to the Cape.

The invention of the pivoting centerboard by a British naval officer in 1809 proved a boon to the packet trade. By the 1820s, they were in use on vessels on Cape Cod Bay. "Centerboards had great effect on American commercial vessels for they not only allowed shallow draft for coastal waters but would sail well when light, and handled smartly in confined situations," according to Mahoney. Captain Jesse Collins was said to use the first centerboard sloop in Eastham in 1824, between sails to Boston to sell salt for "five or six cents per bushel," Mahoney wrote.

Mahoney thinks sometime during the 1820s a wooden mast (or pole) was planted alongside the scrub oaks in Yarmouth on Germans Hill, where Station Avenue and Route 6 now intersect. Twice a week a local lad would "run a red-painted barrel to the mast peak," signaling to folks on the south side that the north side packets were about to hit dock. "The packet sloop *Betsey* with Captain Ansel Hallet at the wheel, would be rounding Sandy Neck and tacking for the Bass Hole landing on its regular schedule from Boston." Blackball Hill in Dennis served the same purpose, alerting folks on the South side to begin their journey to the bay to pick up provisions or passengers.

Around 1830, Captain Zoheth Rich of Truro, a veteran skipper of the packet *Comet*, had an idea that would turn the Cape Cod packet trade on its ears. Since most everyone knew sailing to China was quicker and safer than traveling to Boston by land, why not, Captain Rich thought, build a first-rate packet vessel? Not a plucky, sparse schooner, the type that had been ferrying people and goods back and forth to Boston for shopping, visiting and business, but a gorgeous, comfortable vessel. He built the vessel *Post boy* with cabins constructed of solid mahogany and draperies sewn from imported bolts of silk. Rarely was a cabin empty.

The heyday of Cape Cod packets stretched across much of the nineteenth century, from just after the War of 1812 to about 1875. Not until the Old Colony Railroad first came to Cape Cod in 1848 and progressed slowly eastward with its permanent railroad spikes along the spine of Cape Cod did packets have a transportation rival. Even the modern steam engines that replaced weather-dependent sailing vessels were no match for the railroad.

Before packets, travel to Boston meant hitching a ride as a lone passenger on anything that floated, like a fishing schooner. The alternative by land was a gruesome stagecoach ride: dirty, bumpy and long. Given a choice, Cape Codders, as the old adage goes, preferred "salt to dust." But launching a packet on the bay side was tough, given erratic tides in Brewster, Orleans and Eastham. With their deep harbors, Provincetown and Truro packets sailed on a regular schedule, but all other packets did not. Packet captains would rest vessels on their sides until the tides came in and then sail to Boston.

Local newspapers carried ads listing the hours and routes of stagecoaches to get packet travelers from Orleans, Brewster, Chatham, Harwich and other Lower Cape communities out to the scheduled packets in Provincetown and Truro. Men like Captain Charles Goodspeed, who strolled the decks of his packet vessel the steamer *Naushon* when it sailed from Provincetown to Boston in June 1852, made out like bandits. Every Monday, Wednesday and Friday, promptly at 9:00 a.m., the *Naushon* left Provincetown, returning from Eastern Steam Boat Wharf in Boston on alternating mornings. A round-trip ticket was under three dollars and meals cost twenty-five cents.

Coastal packets made efficient training schools for freshman sailors, who learned simple but necessary sea trades and within the year might find themselves in the forecastle of a

Billingsgate Lighthouse once graced Cape Cod Bay. *Courtesy of the William Brewster Nickerson Memorial Room, Cape Cod Community College.*

brigantine off the coast of China. Sometimes, though, travel by packet was as thrilling as watching paint dry on a picket fence. In the days before steam, when there was no wind, there was no sail.

Just ask young Albert Smith. On a feverishly hot July morning in 1847, minutes before 9:00 a.m., the fifteen-year-old boarded the packet schooner *President Washington*, leaving Boston for Orleans in Cape Cod Bay. Minutes later, the schooner, without a shred of wind, drifted with the tide, and the captain anchored the vessel. A paltry breeze sprang up but didn't so much as sneeze into her sails. Folks started getting restless. A boat was lowered so the passengers—our young Smith presumably among them—could row to a nearby island for fun until sunset. By nightfall, with hours of sailing ahead, the twenty-five passengers were getting tired, and slept in shifts to share the ten available bunks. One group dozed until midnight, then promptly roused out of sleep and turned their accommodations over to the next shift. By morning, all onboard were dismayed to learn they were a good twenty-four hours from Orleans.

A small but respectable shipbuilding company in North Yarmouth (Yarmouth Port was not incorporated until 1828) was installed at Bray Farm off Chase Garden Creek. Today Bray Farm is owned by the Town of Yarmouth and is preserved as a historic landmark. It's worth visiting if you get the chance. Schooners and sloops between 60 to 150 tons went off the ways at Chase Garden, Mahoney wrote.

In the late 1830s, fresh from learning the shipbuilding trade in Boston and Maine, young Asa Shiverick Jr. came home to East Dennis, to the banks of Sesuit Neck, where his father built fishing schooners and packet sloops. Asa Jr. settled into the family business with brothers David and Paul. By day for most of the 1840s, Asa Jr. and his brothers worked alongside their dad and churned out no fewer than five vessels, ideal for fishing and the coastal packet trade. By night, though, talk at the supper table centered on the new species of vessel—the clipper—that had ignited a fever of obsession in the tightly knit maritime community the world over.

The first clippers were built in the 1840s in New York City. "They were the fastest, most beautiful wooden sailing vessels the world had ever seen," one observer noted. "Long and lean, with sharp bows, raked masts and a great cumulus of sail." In those days, the only way to move commercial goods and people between foreign ports was by tall ship, and whoever got to their destinations the fastest, especially to China and the West Indies, won the money and prestige. With the California Gold Rush in September 1848 came a new sense of urgency to transport food, manufactured goods and equipment around Cape Horn from the East Coast to San Francisco, where the population grew by hundreds daily.

Clearly the manufacture of clipper ships was the cutting edge in maritime technology in the 1840s. The Shivericks wondered could, should, this small family shipyard in this backward little village on Cape Cod dare to compete against larger, established shipyards in East Boston, New York and Maine? There was only one way to find out. And the planning, nineteenth-century style, began. Keep the business in the family—father and sons decided—keep the family business in the village, surround themselves with skilled, loyal craftsmen and financiers and secure the flow of building materials and manufactured goods needed to produce the ships.

The dream took hold on the floor of a meadow overlooking Sesuit Creek in 1849. Later that year, in July, the 546-ton *Revenue* was launched into Cape Cod Bay. As soon as the *Revenue* was launched, work on the *Hippogriffe* began. It was launched in 1852, and was slightly larger than the *Revenue*. The Shiverick brothers produced five medium and three extreme clippers between 1850 and 1862, each new one slightly larger than the last. Captain Anthony Howes of East Dennis sailed the *Hippogriffe* to San Francisco on its maiden voyage. (Seven years later, the vessel hit an uncharted rock in the Java Sea, and today Hippogriffe Rock is still on the charts.) The *Belle of the West* and the *Kit Carson* were launched in 1853 and 1854, respectively. The *Wild Hunter* came off the ways in 1855, followed by the *Christopher Hall* in 1858 and the *Ellen Sears* in 1863. The Shivericks also constructed the *Searsville*, a coastwise schooner, in 1854.

Though none set any record for speed, the vessels were tight as drums, and every ship that came off the ways was a beauty. The Shiverick brothers had succeeded. Even prestigious Boston shipyards grew to respect the tiny outfit on a shallow creek in East Dennis. In the end, despite natural business acumen, Asa Jr., David and Paul were plain lucky. Though they created their own opportunity in a Yankee market craving fast ships, fate had timed the start of their clipper endeavor perfectly. The new-and-improved, second-generation shipyard paralleled the so-called Great Age of Sail, when tall ships dominated the global market. Had they waited even five or ten years, the venture would have collapsed and fallen the way of the numerous failed dot-coms whose remains litter the economic landscape of today. And when the bottom fell out of the clipper ship industry—when railroads and steam engines rendered the tall ships obsolete—the Shivericks knew when to hang up the hammer, with little or no debt, fat, happy and retired, to East Dennis, of course.

Supporting the Shipbuilding Industry

If Cape Cod seamen—the whalers, fishermen and merchant mariners—from the seventeenth and into the twentieth centuries were the envy of the maritime world, they were so only by the sweat, imagination and dignity of land-bound craftsmen and women. They included the women whose hands tirelessly wove the cloth for their shirts, the tailor whose needle fashioned black suits and top hats for captains and trousers for seamen, the village cooper whose oaken barrels held their dried cranberries, the farmer who grew the rye for their supper bread or the carpenter who constructed simple but sturdy flakes on which the flesh of salted fish would dry in the sun. Their work may not have been seen by consumers of Cape exports, but in an indirect way it was as important to driving the local economy during any stage of the nineteenth century as the sailor who raised canvas.

About 1824, David Snow of Orleans baked batches of sea biscuits and sheets of spicy gingerbread, and for $1.50 a barrel, he sold the foodstuffs to cooks stocking galleys on vessels in Chatham's fishing fleet, whaling vessels based in Provincetown and vessels transiting Cape Cod Bay. Benjamin Walker and Joel Clark owned two of the fifty saltworks that sprouted up in Eastham along the north side along Cape Cod Bay, and near the

The *Searsville* was constructed by the Shiverick brothers in their East Dennis shipyard. *Courtesy of the Dennis Historical Society.*

town cove at Salt Pond. By the end of 1837, the vats—using the sun to evaporate their contents—yielded 22,370 bushels of salt and much of that was shipped off-Cape.

Homespun nets enabled fishing fleets to harvest quintals (one quintal equals one hundred pounds) of cod from local waters. In 1845, Provincetown reported twenty thousand quintals, with Chatham a close second at fifteen thousand and down the line that year, town by town, with Eastham taking home a modest three hundred quintals.

Soon after Cyrus Cahoon cultivated some of the first cranberry crops on Pleasant Lake in Harwich about 1847, a portion of the native fruit would naturally find its way onto the deck of a local vessel. The British had their limes to combat scurvy; local farmers gave Yankee sailors the cranberry.

From the town of Yarmouth came rope made in one of two ropewalks, buildings some eight hundred feet in length, gone long before the advent of photography. After the demise of local ropewalks, Cape outfitters ordered from the Plymouth Cordage Company, just across Cape Cod Bay, close enough to almost be from 'home,' and far from the jungles of India from whose botanical corridors the raw jute was harvested and brought back to the Cape for processing. Provisioning vessels was steady work. A ship needed tiny, iron nails fashioned by blacksmiths and coopers to handcraft oaken barrels, into which local pond water would be drawn to quench a sailor's thirst halfway around the world.

Once in a while a land-bound merchant would rise above his working-class roots to gain the prestige and money generally reserved for sea captains or ship owners he had often served. Remember our young David Snow of Orleans? Once up to his elbows in flour as a lad in his early days, Snow, who died in 1875 at the age of seventy-seven, was by his fifties a wealthy merchant in Boston who owned not only trading ships, but also three piers at which his vessels were docked: Constitution, Arches and Packard Wharves. Indeed, Snow is credited with having cornered the salt and fish trade in all of New England during the 1850s. Not bad for a young lad who started out baking biscuits.

Toward the end of the Great Age of Sail, many clippers and other wooden vessels were converted to barges or were dismantled and their wood was used for houses and other projects.

Cape Cod Bay did not have a harbor deep enough, with the possible exception of Provincetown Harbor, to support a lively sea trade with vessels such as a barkentine or bark. But Cape Cod Bay was home to many sea captains who sailed the world and dreamed of coming home safely. Brewster was known as a hotspot for producing sea captains. In 1850, over fifty captains lived in that town. In *Cape Cod, Masters of the Seas*, Joan Paine wrote:

> *It just could be that this rate of success in Shipmastering was due in part to Brewster's pioneering school system. Parson Simpkins went on to say that "the residents have for some years maintained a man's school throughout the year...they regularly subscribe $3,000 toward the academy's support." The "man's school" would have given Brewster boys intensive courses in astronomy, navigation, mathematics, chart making and reading, and probably a good grounding in trading and money management.*

Ever glorious, though, as being a captain was, the position held loneliness close to its vest. Pain and longing gripped the heart of Captain Henry Knowles. "I don't know when I have felt so utterly lonely and sad," mused the Brewster shipmaster. "How miserable I feel." Captain Knowles wrote in his diary before retiring aboard the *Belle Creole* of Boston as the vessel left Scotland in the dead of the winter of 1865, bound for the Indian Ocean. As the vessel swayed against the frigid waves of the North Atlantic, to his diary the thirty-one-year-old revealed a mood black as the coal in the cargo hold.

"Yet it is well, for if this separation has learned me to be more kind and affectionate to her, for I know now how dearly I love her," noted Knowles. Greatly missing his young wife, Lizzie, and daughter, Grace Pacific—so named for her birth at sea two years before—had sent this usually affable skipper into a slight depression. "Last night when I came below to retire I looked at my bed now vacant, 'o, dear,' I said, 'what would I not give to have Lizzie here.'"

Knowles was a man who at a young age realized the worth of a simple embrace. Absolutely one senses that Captain Knowles appreciated every nuance of his wife's personality as each lonely day passed. "I sigh for her presence," he wrote in early February 1865, "I think how I would endeavor to please her by kind and endearing words and acts."

During the voyage, which lasted eight months, Knowles passed his spare time reading the Bible. On nearly every page of his diary a religious reference is intermingled with a prayer for Lizzie and Grace Pacific. "I daily pray to him to protect my dear wife and child from all diseases and harm of whatsoever nature and kind." Lonely though he may have been, Knowles was still a captain with layers of duty and responsibility, and he found solace in knowing that at least the voyage was, so far and excuse the pun, smooth sailing. "Everything goes on pleasantly on board. I have not yet heard an unkind word spoken by anyone," so reads the diary. "I have a good crew, good officers, and I hope, cook and Steward."

Missing in some researchers' notes is the human price paid to this job that required travel over watery roadways and months at a stretch away from home. The pain of the separation from other humans they loved. The uncertainty mariners' wives felt when their husbands left home for many months at a time: would they return alive and well? The months passed and thankfully Henry went home, alive and well, by late September 1865, reunited with his beloved Lizzie and Grace Pacific.

Henry and Lizzie Knowles would have six more children, and by all indications had a long and happy marriage. Henry Knowles commanded the *Belle Creole* until 1869, when seawater leaked into its hull, expanded the cargo of guano—bird droppings—and sank the vessel in the Atlantic. After that, Knowles came ashore and never went to sea again. In 1870, the former shipmaster moved his family to Rockford, Illinois. (Why specifically there is a mystery.) Knowles took up the grocery business, becoming a moderately successful wholesaler of butter, cheese and eggs. There he died on January 27, 1893. His wife, Lizzie, lived until 1905.

Low tide at Yarmouth Port. *Courtesy of the Historical Society of Old Yarmouth.*

Barnstable Customs House

During the Revolutionary War, the British collected import levies in a red brick, Italianate-style building in today's Coast Guard Heritage Museum at the Trayser along Route 6A in Barnstable village. Following the war, the building became a government customs collections house where taxes were collected under the new Department of the Treasury and Secretary Alexander Hamilton, beginning in September 1789. "At Hamilton's insistence customs districts were established in all the original states. The Cape Cod district was one of the first created," wrote Francis Broadhurst in *A History of the U.S. Custom House and Post Office Building*. "It was headquartered in the village of Barnstable, the Shiretown for Barnstable County, and one of the busiest ports in New England." The first collector for Customs District VII was General Joseph Otis of West Barnstable, a local Revolutionary War hero.

Family Life along Cape Cod Bay

In March 1830, forty-six-year-old Jaazaniah Gross of Truro, a well-respected sea captain from an established clan, fell deathly ill with a "malignant fever" and died five days later. When little Marianne Hallett, daughter of the famed Captain Bangs Hallett, lay dying of dysentery in 1846, caregivers lovingly attended to the three-year-old from Yarmouth Port until her last breath.

Death and dying fill the pages of nearly every book on Cape Cod history, and few families in the nineteenth century escaped losing a loved one to maladies that would never grace the chart of a local doctor today: consumption, typhoid, smallpox, diphtheria and typhus. Frantic family members may have called on a doctor to attend these stricken Cape Codders, but physicians were scarce and anyway, methods used to heal were well within the reach of lay caregivers who relied on herbs, vegetables and even folk wisdom passed through generations. "Most of the time when someone got sick, it would have been someone in their family, their household, to give the primary care," said Christie Higginbottom, a research historian at Old Sturbridge Village, a recreated 1830 New England farming community.

"Nursing was done by family members," clarified Jim Owens, a retired Eastham schoolteacher with an extensive background in local history. He said extended family like grandparents tended their own sick brood and their experience in doing so equaled "a lot of wisdom passed down from one generation to another."

Cape Cod had physicians but one, maybe two doctors per town. Indeed, in 1890 twenty physicians claimed membership in the Barnstable District Medical Society. Caregivers connect the linen and wool–covered sickbed of the 1800s to today's hospital emergency rooms, be they professionals with medical degrees or family members who put untrained but concerned hands over the feverish brows of children. In the end, no matter who it was that hovered over a sickbed, what specific care could the sick and dying be offered in an age before antibiotics, in the days before scientists linked disease to dirt and bacteria?

"People kept around them a supply of herbs they grew," explained Higginbottom, who said that besides turning to the backyard garden Cape Codders "could always purchase things at a store" or apothecary. Many old-time remedies are in some form used today, though most from yesteryear treated the symptoms of an illness or disease, not the unknown cause. For instance, colds were treated with sage herbal tea or simply by pouring boiling water into the leaves from a sage plant, letting the mixture steep and then straining and serving it. Gargling sage tea helped soothe a sore throat. Sugared caraway seeds or sugared fennel seeds helped prevent indigestion. Ginger root eased an upset stomach.

"What people observed was typically when you're sick, there's some change in the humors," said Higginbottom. "If you have a fever, you get flushed, if you have the flu, you cough up phlegm." Sickness also fit the patterns of changes in bowel movements and urine. We trace the old adage "he's not in good humor" to this theory. When body humors were in balance, physicians were taught and lay caregivers presumed, one is in good health. Common medical thinking in the early to mid-nineteenth century dictated that the body, or nature, tried to correct this imbalance of fluids by evacuating a fluid, and remedies were given to aid this process.

"If a child has a fever, the caregiver would presume the imbalance is in the head, and that to remedy the situation you'd want to draw the humors down more evenly through the body, so warmed onions would be applied, bound to the soles of feet, to draw out the fever," said Higginbottom. An onion was considered a draught, which means to pull or draw, she explained.

Another mindset came from medicine itself: if it imitated the illness it will cure the illness, too. "Its use has a clear logic," asserted Higginbottom. "People had observed patients with fevers, and they saw just before the fever broke, the patient would break out into a sweat. So if you gave medication to force the sweat, they believed it would break the fever."

Along with health issues, keeping warm was a great concern for families on Cape Cod, especially those near the bay, where unforgiving winds battered the shore. In truth, so much wood was taken from the shores of Cape Cod Bay that one could stand on Route 6A, then known only as Main Street, for a perfect view of the water. During a cold snap in 1844, Brewster shopkeeper Isaac Dillingham, whose store was not far from Cape Cod Bay, ran a sale on wood stoves in late January, when for at least one night across the state the temperature hovered at twenty-two degrees below zero. With the possible exception of water, Cape Codders valued seasoned firewood—winter's gold—above any other natural resource. Keeping your average Cape Cod home or business warm and toasty 160 years ago was itself a part-time, daily job. It required special skills and patience, unlike today, where merely throwing a switch to turn on the natural gas or oil heating systems is necessary.

"By the 1840s with the fast-growing availability and popularity of stoves, many families began to heat more than just the kitchen and perhaps one other room," said Frank White, curator of mechanical arts at Old Sturbridge Village. He said Cape Codders would have set up stoves in their parlors and maintained fires in them on all but the coldest days. "The center of family activity was no longer the large open fireplace in the kitchen around which all the members gathered on cold winter evenings," said White. People started putting wood stoves in the middle of the room, thus warming the space more evenly. "Their activities, sewing, reading, playing, were moved to other parts of the room and were lighted by portable lamps since the fire had ceased to be the most important source of light in the room," he added.

Compared to fireplaces, wood stoves were a grand leap in efficiency, and, said White, reduced the amount of heat loss, especially if they were placed out in the room and were connected to the chimney with a stovepipe. "With this kind of installation both the cast iron of the stove and the sheet iron of the pipe radiated heat into the room." But gathering around the fireplace was a time-honored tradition that Cape Codders had a hard time letting go of. "Some estimates suggest that a family could reduce the consumption of firewood by 50 to 75 percent by replacing their large cooking fireplace with a cast iron cooking stove that would also be a good source of heat."

In a well-run home, firewood would have been prepped the preceding winter so it could dry and season, and first thing in the morning, either the father of the house or an older son would carry the wood inside and stack it in the firebox, though it fell to women to keep the home fires burning, literally, during the day. "The wood for fueling stoves was usually cut into four-foot lengths and carried by ox or horse-drawn sled from the woods to the farmyard," said White. "The four-foot lengths might be split into quarters in the woods or in the yard and then stacked outdoors to dry through the summer."

How much firewood was necessary varied from house to house, depending on its size, how many people were in a family and whether that family used a fireplace or wood stove. Some households burned up to forty cords in a year for cooking and heating. An 1846 survey of firewood consumption in Massachusetts households—according to White—gives a low of four cords and a high of over thirty cords per household and places the average at about thirty cords. (A cord measures 128 cubic feet and is normally stacked 4 feet high, 4 feet deep and 8 feet long. To give you an idea how much wood is in a cord, one cord could build thirty Boston rockers, or manufacture 942 one-pound books.)

These measures helped conserve fuel, but none compared to the need for wood. But when burned, what was meant to soothe and protect also killed. In its February 1, 1844 edition, *The Yarmouth Register* carried a story from its rival, the *Barnstable Patriot*, of a child of Patty Crocker in West Barnstable along Cape Cod Bay who died of burns. "The little sufferer—a boy of 2½ years—had been left alone for a considerable time in a room where there was a fire, and when its mother returned she found it standing in the middle of the floor, with its clothes on fire, and the child so dreadfully burned as to survive the accident but a short time."

Concord's Ambassador

His was the most famous trip to Cape Cod ever written about, except, perhaps, for the first string of European explorers in the early seventeenth century. In 1849, when Cape Cod was just finding its sturdy feet in commercial industries and joining the rest of Massachusetts, Henry David Thoreau arrived. Indeed, he was especially fond of oysters.

Nearly all the oyster shops and stands in Massachusetts, I am told, are supplied and kept by natives of Wellfleet, and a part of this town is still called Billingsgate from the oysters having been formerly planted there, but the native oysters are said to have died in 1770. Various causes are assigned to this, such as a ground frost, the carcasses of blackfish kept to rot in the harbor, and the like, but the most common account of the matter is (and I find that a similar superstition with regard to the disappearance of fishes exists almost everywhere) that when Wellfleet began to quarrel with the neighboring towns about the right to gather them, yellow specks appeared in them, and Providence caused them to disappear. A few years ago sixty thousand bushels were annually brought from the South and planted in the harbor of Wellfleet till they attained "the proper relish of Billingsgate"; but now they are imported commonly full-grown and laid down near their markets at Boston and elsewhere, where the water, being a mixture of salt and fresh, suits them better.

Even more so than Barnstable Harbor, its lovely but lowlier cousin, the ever-vibrant Provincetown Harbor captured Thoreau's imagination and admiration. "It opens to the south, is free from rocks, and is never frozen over. It is said that the only ice seen in it drifts in sometimes from Barnstable or Plymouth."

Underground Railroad and the Civil War

Very little data exist to confirm that Yankee sea captains used Cape Cod Bay to ferry escaped slaves to freedom to points north. It's tantamount to the Viking question: much speculation and nothing concrete, but it's more than probable marine conductors used Cape Cod Bay on their northern route.

Cape Codders contributed to the underground railroad through the Vigilance Committee in Boston. Appointed by a "public meeting" at Faneuil Hall in October 1850, the committee accepted donations to ferry escaped slaves to the North by ship, rail or coach. Judging by the ledger maintained by Treasurer Francis Jackson, a handful of Cape Codders gave money to the cause. In 1851, the Reverend Giles Pease of Sandwich contributed $6 and in July 1854 the cleric again donated, this time $8.50 to the cause. It is probable but not conclusively proven that vessels used Cape Cod Bay to transport clients on the underground railroad, but improbable to think they did not.

Captain Austin Bearse was a mate on ships active in the slave trade in the South. Once home, Bearse joined the Vigilance Committee and acted as its general agent. "He served as doorkeeper at the secret meetings, and he used his yacht, the *Wild Pigeon*, to help carry fugitives to safety," according to author Irving Bartlett.

In a letter to Captain Bearse dated January 10, 1853, Wendell Phillips asked for help for the safe passage of a slave boy named Bernardo:

Dear Friend

When my little colored boy arrives, I wish you to take charge of him, and keep him till you Can get some safe way to send him to the Cape. You know it is not safe to have colored

In the 1850s, over two hundred people lived at the Long Point Settlement overlooking Provincetown Harbor. *Courtesy of the William Brewster Nickerson Memorial Room, Cape Cod Community College.*

children Travelling about alone, so be very careful that you get him to a safe conveyance. He is to be sent to J.E. Mayo, Harwich, to stop at the Union store there. If Mr. Mayo is not there, Captain Small will attend to him.

Bernardo made the trip safely. Abolitionists boasted that an escaped slave could make it from the South to Canada inside of forty-eight hours, and to think of doing so without the aid of sail, given Cape Cod Bay's strategic position along the Massachusetts coast, might be foolish.

The Civil War did not engage Cape Cod Bay as a battlefield, but scores of Cape Cod men enlisted to lend their maritime skills to the Union cause and serve at key battle sites in the South. Captain Levi Crowell of West Dennis was captured by the Thirteenth Georgia Regiment and spent five months in a Confederate prison in 1862. Among the many other Cape Codders who served were Charles I. Gibbs of Sandwich and William U. Grozier of Provincetown. Grozier received command of the ironclad *Nausett*, which left Boston on August 9, 1865, about four months after the Civil War ended. "In what appears to be the only instance of a Civil War ironclad making port on the Cape, he brought her into Provincetown Harbor on August 12, where she was a big attraction, her log noting 'a large number of citizens from the shore visited the ship,'" wrote Stauffer Miller in *Hoisting Their Colors: Cape Cod's Civil War Navy Officers*.

The government took note of the strategic position of the Sandy Neck Lighthouse, which is sometimes called the Beach Point Lighthouse. A long line of Baxter clan members served as keeper, according to historian Stauffer Miller.

A Union fortification built at Long Point on Provincetown Harbor didn't see one bullet fired during the Civil War. Called Fort Useless and Fort Ridiculous by locals, these defense posts overlooking Provincetown Harbor were built because a Confederate warship was once spotted near Provincetown.

Cape Cod Bay was relatively quiet during the Civil War.

CHAPTER SEVEN

PROGRESS AND A NEW CENTURY

The nation behaves well if it treats the natural resources as assets which it must turn over to the next generation increased; and not impaired in value.
—*Theodore Roosevelt*

The *Alice May Davenport*

Locals called 1905 a "four-quilt winter." A cold snap froze a good chunk of Cape Cod Bay during a nor'easter in late January, encasing two new wooden schooners in ice off the belly of the bay. The *Alice May Davenport* of Bath, Maine, sat immobile off North Dennis. A bit farther west, near Lone Tree Creek in Yarmouth Port, the five-masted *Harwood Palmer* met the same icy fate. According to historian Noel Beyle, "Both vessels had tried to ride out the gale at anchor [each with a cargo of coal], but their anchor chains parted, and they went aground on Jan. 25, 1905—eventually trapped for the duration of the winter in ice that measured eight feet thick in spots."

The *Davenport*, on its maiden voyage, wouldn't be freed until March 21, and of all the ironies of that date, the first day of spring! It then continued on, bound for Newport News, Virginia, with its cargo of coal intact. The *Harwood Palmer* wasn't so lucky. The sweat of men and horses, plus a few tugs, according to Beyle, were needed to nudge the *Palmer* from its icy berth. Later, a dredger dug a deep-water channel that allowed the four-master to finally get out of Cape Cod Bay on May 20, 1905, also bound for Newport News.

Hundreds of vessels, large and small, have wrecked in Cape Cod Bay or sustained serious damage because of bad weather conditions such as nor'easters and ice storms, or poor seamanship that landed a vessel on a shoal or into rocks. "The granite lighters *Benjamin Franklin* and *Potomac* were driven ashore at Sandwich in a northeast gale on November 9, 1909," wrote William Quinn in *Cape Cod Maritime Disasters*. "The two lighters with 23 crewmen on board were part of a group of vessels engaged in laying a breakwater for the new Cape Cod Canal," he added. Both vessels were total losses.

In November 1920, the USS *Swan*, a former minesweeper, stranded in Cape Cod Bay; sixty-three people were rescued and the vessel was later towed toward a beach by a

The *Alice May Davenport* lies embedded in ice off North Dennis in 1905. *Courtesy of Mrs. Susan Davenport, Bass River.*

salvage company. The floor of Cape Cod Bay is littered with the iron bones and wooden shards of past shipwrecks.

In her book, *Dennis Cape Cod*, Nancy Thacher Reid recounted how Dennis native Joshua Crowell remembered how his father, Nathan, assisted neighbors and townsfolk free the *Davenport*:

> *1905 was in the era when horses were the main motive power and many farmers and other tradesmen had "sand plows."* [A sand plow was described by Beyle as a horse-drawn scoop used to move sand and dirt before the advent of bulldozers and front-end loaders.] *Father, together with other men, used their horses and sand plows, at low tide, to scoop away sand around the schooner and to excavate a shallow channel across the flats toward what would be deep water at high tide. Apparently this maneuver was successful enough to allow the schooner to float and get back into the deep water at high tide.*

Unlike the War of 1812 and the notorious British blockade, and the times privateers skirted British patrols in the American Revolution, Cape Cod Bay saw little action in World War I, except as a staging area and support region for troops on their way to Europe. Tragically, eighty-one years ago an American submarine collided with a Coast Guard destroyer off Provincetown on December 17, 1927, and forty men died as a result.

The USCGC *Paulding* cut in front of the S-boat, unaware of its presence. "Water gushed into the battery room through the 2½ foot-by-1-foot hole as the vessel sank more than 100 feet to the ocean floor," reported the *Boston Herald* in 2007. Forty sailors survived the actual collision, but thirty-four soon died. Six survivors trapped in the torpedo room used Morse code to communicate with rescuers. They suffocated. Their final transmission to the would-be rescue team: "We understand."

"It was the most traumatic marine accident in Provincetown history, and riveted the country for days because some of the crewmen remained alive in a small hold of the sub, tapping morse code against the hull, heard by divers," according to Seth Rolbein, editor and publisher of *The Cape Cod Voice*. "The fishermen of the town were incensed because they believed they could have rescued the sub faster than the U.S. government, but were not allowed to make the attempt," Rolbein added.

Rumrunners and Prohibition

During the years of Prohibition—January 6, 1919, to December 5, 1933—when the federal government restricted alcohol consumption and distribution, Cape Codders drank anyway, as did the rest of the nation. The real action was on Nantucket Sound, where authorities confiscated hundreds of vessels carrying alcohol against the spirit of the 18th Amendment to the Constitution.

Cape Cod Bay was a quieter and occasional distribution route. On Wednesday, May 25, 1925, the Coast Guard apprehended the notorious *Peg II* off Ellisville in Sandwich while it lay in at the dock there. Six hundred bags of Scotch, gin and champagne, valued at $2,887.40, were confiscated. Only at dock was the Coast Guard able to catch up with the vessel, which sported two four-hundred-horsepower airplane engines, giving the *Peg II* a top speed of forty-five miles an hour.

Darkness had set in on Plymouth Harbor on Saturday, January 10, 1925, when Coast Guard Boatswain Mate Antone Lema, on patrol near Bug-Light, saw a boat at anchor about five hundred yards away. As he approached, two men jumped into a small dory and began rowing toward the beach. The tide was too low for Lema to follow, but with the attached government dory deployed, Lema caught up with the duo and then both parties rowed back to the larger vessels. "When they got back, I asked them to take up one of the Hatches, which they did, and I plainly saw a number of barrels marked Scotch malt," recounted Lema. All told, twenty-eight barrels of prime Scotch malt were confiscated.

Forty-five minutes later, after Plymouth Police took the rumrunners into custody, Lema saw another boat coming into the channel south of Bug-Light. He investigated and found three hundred cases of alcohol aboard. Two more men were arrested and turned over to Plymouth Police.

H.O. Daniels was the officer in charge of the Cahoon's Hollow Coast Guard Station in Wellfleet. In a November 23, 1927, letter to the district office, Daniels said he suspected the motor boat *Ethel E. Young* of being a rumrunner with operations based on Billingsgate Island off Wellfleet in the bay. A Captain Tulk said he intended to set up a winter fishing station at Billingsgate, but, as Daniels wrote, "Before I enlisted in the Coast Guard, I put in three winters at Billingsgate Island, and I know that it is impossible for any man to be there alone, in any boat, and make wages during the winter, fishing. As this move looks suspicious too [*sic*] me, I am letting you know just what has happened."

The Cape Cod Canal and World War II

Miles Standish thought it would be a good idea, and so did George Washington: build a canal to link Buzzards Bay to Cape Cod Bay. In fact, Washington had a survey made in 1791 by a Cambridge engineer.

"Like all great canals, Suez or Panama, possibilities were seen long before they were realized, thousands of years for Suez, hundreds for Panama, and generations for Cape Cod," wrote Albert Perry Brigham of Colgate University. The Cape Cod Canal, he wrote, "has already become one of the most important waterways of the Atlantic coast and a part of that great system of protected channels by which communication will, in the near future, be established between our Northern and Southern shores."

Private business dealings to construct a canal were successful, but it wasn't until the federal government assumed control and reconstructed the canal during the Depression years that the canal became what it is today. It now consists of three bridges, and the channel was deepened and widened, the lighting system was improved and the bank revetment was replaced.

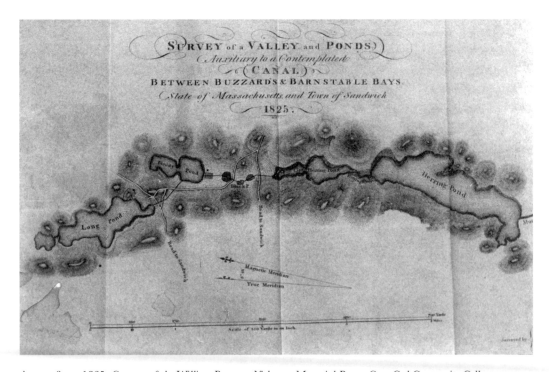

A map from 1825. *Courtesy of the William Brewster Nickerson Memorial Room, Cape Cod Community College.*

A map of Cape Cod Bay from U.S. Coast Guard District 1. *Courtesy of the William Brewster Nickerson Memorial Room, Cape Cod Community College.*

In 2006, nearly 13,883 vessels sailed or motored through the Cape Cod Canal, a sea-level, 17.4-mile federal navigation project extending from Cleveland Ledge Light in Buzzards Bay to Cape Cod Bay. The canal is what makes Cape Cod an island, not the natural peninsula glaciers carved. "This 480-foot wide by 32-foot deep canal provides a mileage savings of 65 to 166 miles for vessels that would otherwise have to travel around the historically treacherous outer shores of Cape Cod," said Samantha Mirabella, a park ranger and member of the U.S. Army Corps of Engineers who conducts educational programs on the canal.

Cargo barges, container ships, recreational and commercial fishing boats, sailboats and charter vessels meander through the wickedly strong currents, all under the watchful gaze of the U.S. Army Corps of Engineers.

The Cape Cod Canal provided European-bound American military convoys safe transit away from enemy subs south of Cape Cod in World War II. To protect the critical waterway from Germans, the army built a Coastal Fortification in Sagamore at the canal's eastern entrance in 1941. The 241st Coast Artillery Battery C called the encampment home, which consisted of six barracks, one canteen and a slew of small outbuildings. After the war, the army dismantled the compound and now the area is back to its natural state, mostly forest, swamp and some fields.

Today, the U.S. Coast Guard maintains a keen presence on Cape Cod Bay, with an air station at Otis Air National Guard Base and, on the bay side, stations in Sandwich and Provincetown.

A quahaug crew quietly at work in Cape Cod Bay. *Courtesy of Stanley and Bonnie Snow, Orleans.*

The Target Ship

The SS *James Longstreet*, a $1.8 million Liberty Ship launched in Houston in October 1942, carried dry goods on three international voyages in World War II, to Australia, Canada and India, to name a few ports. A storm one year later off Sandy Hook, New Jersey, south of New York City, wrecked the 441-foot vessel. The navy hauled the mortally wounded ship to Cape Cod Bay for use as target practice. Today what remains of the *Longstreet*, named for a Confederate war hero, lies in about 25 feet of water on New Found Shoal about 3.5 miles off Eastham and north of Orleans.

And speaking of Orleans, Noel W. Beyle insists that the Campbell Soup Company ran its trucks to Rock Harbor to harvest clams for use in soups and chowders in about the 1940s.

Nothing Is Permanent Except Change

The appearance of the water sheet itself might not have been distorted much over the centuries, but changes to the shoreline over the generations are unmistakable. Nearly the entire perimeter of Cape Cod Bay has been altered by the hands of human advancement, industry, recreation and other commercial ventures and uses.

This and next page: Pilot whales or blackfish after a mass stranding in Wellfleet. *Courtesy of Marcella Curry, Sturgis Library.*

A few years after the beginning of the twentieth century, attitudes on behalf of marine conservation remained largely unchanged. Indeed, the bursting field of cetacean conservation hardly flickered in the eyes of Wellfleet's citizens a century ago. The rotting carcasses of dozens of bloating, headless blackfish—the old Cape Cod name for pilot whales—cluttered a beach at Wellfleet in early October 1912. The heads of slaughtered mammals, jaws falsely "smiling" open in the early fall air, are lined up in the bloody sand. With the gently sloping areas mixed with extreme tides, pilot whales found little haven in Wellfleet Harbor.

The blackfish had beached themselves and locals wasted no time in divvying up the catch for blubber from which to render oil, as good as cold cash in those days. Wellfleet and pilot shore whaling go way back. Pilgrims in October 1620 caught a glimpse of a dozen or so Native Americans skinning a dead blackfish that stranded itself in Billingsgate Bay, later Wellfleet Harbor, near what is today the Wellfleet-Eastham boundary. Even before the Revolutionary War, most of Wellfleet's men who worked the maritime trades did so in whaling. "In 1771 Wellfleet is credited with having 30 whalers of 75 tons, each employing 15 men," wrote Everett Nye in *A History of Wellfleet*, published in 1920.

Mass strandings were recorded through the nineteenth century, and as one historian claimed, word of a beaching would empty church pews and schools. Mass strandings were incredibly welcome to the local economy during fishing's off-seasons. What the sea threw their way, people used to live on and sustain their families, whether by selling its rich oil or eating whale meat. For decades the slaughter continued whenever nature mysteriously steered blackfish off course toward land, or if a pilot whale was caught unawares by a tricky tide, wrapped up like a present and hand delivered to those onshore to a sure and acceptable death. Just a few weeks after the October 1912 stranding at Wellfleet, a local newspaper reported "blackfish schools filled the Provincetown Harbor from Long Point to Truro."

Fresh data on whales radically shifted Americans' mindset from slaughter to savior. "The first scientific studies of bottle-nosed dolphins began in 1938, and *National Geographic* published its first of many articles on whales in 1940," noted Mary Malloy, PhD, an author and faculty member in maritime studies at the Sea Education Association in Woods Hole. "In 1967 cetaceans burst fully into the consciousness of Americans when the first killer whale appeared in captivity at the Vancouver Aquarium in British Columbia, and Flipper replaced Lassie as America's favorite and smartest pet," Malloy added. Dolphins in particular, Malloy affirmed, have certainly made an impact on us. "Perennially smiling and obviously intelligent, it's easy to imbue them and their cetacean relations with human characteristics and feelings."

Congress passed the Marine Mammal Protection Act in 1972, making it illegal to harm, harass or kill sea animals like seals, dolphins or pilot whales, to name a few species. Today, pictures of a beachside slaughterhouse revolt us; then, it was the norm. Conservation was unheard of on that fall day in 1912, as a shovel wielded by a cash-hungry Wellfleetian delivered a deathblow to one blackfish after another. Today such actions would be unthinkable.

An Enduring Tradition: The Blessing of the Fleet

Jeremy King is a fisheries biologist with Massachusetts Division of Marine Fisheries. He pointed to two areas of Cape Cod that particularly interest him. "The flats and shallows south of Billingsgate Shoal and into Wellfleet Harbor are warmed by surface water transport from the prevailing southwest wind in summer support a community of fish and invertebrates that is common to the warm waters of Nantucket Sound and uncommon in most of the Gulf of Maine," cited King.

The Provincetown-area waters are equally compelling. "Cape Cod Bay acts like a catch basin for the southern end of the Gulf of Maine. In the fall lots of fish migrate along the eastern shore of the Bay and then exit Cape Cod Bay by passing around Wood End and Race Point. The Provincetown shore sticks out into relatively deep water habitat with a steep drop-off from shore bringing lots of migrating fish close to shore along very narrow bands of preferred depth."

For generations of Provincetown fishing families, it is not the science that evokes communal emotion, it's the tradition of the Blessing of the Fleet. On the last Sunday of June, since 1947, a procession has left St. Joseph's the Apostle Church at noon and wound its way to MacMillan Pier, where a priest, often a bishop, boards a boat to bless what was once a formidable fishing fleet but today are mostly pleasure craft. The procession includes a statue of St. Joseph, the patron saint of fishermen.

A vessel lies mortally wounded in icy waters off Cape Cod Bay. *Courtesy of the William Brewster Nickerson Memorial Room, Cape Cod Community College.*

The blessing has its roots in Portugal and was brought to Gloucester by emigrating fishermen. Arthur Bragg Silva is credited with bringing the fresh tradition to Provincetown after having seen the blessing done in Gloucester. Today, all vessels, even the kayaks, are decked out in banners and ribbons and other finery befitting the rite of passage that the blessing has become.

For decades the late Louie Rivers of Provincetown, who passed on in early 2008, had fished for cod, flounder and "anything that I could catch and sell" off his native Provincetown, a community, he said in an interview several years ago, that would be "lost" without its annual Blessing of the Fleet. "It is a very, very, very religious affair," Rivers, who put net to sea between 1942 and 1982, remembered.

In the old days when P-town's fleet was king, on blessing day there were "seventy-five boats and it took three, four hours," Rivers reminisced. Provincetown honored its fishing culture religiously, literally, without worries about the separation of church and state. Rivers longed for those good old days of fishing, before "all the rules and regulations and all the other crap that goes with it." Over the years, the blessing turned into a four-day Portuguese Festival and there was, Rivers laughed, "an open house on every boat," adding, "within the last ten years it's dwindled considerably, but the spirit is still there."

"Provincetown was built principally from the profits of the salt codfish trade as it was carried on in the 18th and 19th centuries," wrote George Bryant, whose history of the blessing was printed for distribution in 1976. "Provincetown was a fishing town by habit and one that provided a magnificent natural, normally ice-free harbor that was ideal for the maneuvering of sailing vessels and protection from the major oceanic storms."

For years Rivers put out to sea in the *Johnny O*. Then, in 1978 he had the *Miss Sandy* built, named for his daughter, and kept it busy until he retired in 1982. Would he have thought of dropping net without having attended the annual blessing? "I wouldn't even

A map of Long Point. *Courtesy of the William Brewster Nickerson Memorial Room, Cape Cod Community College.*

think about not having it blessed," he said in 2003 from his home in the East End. "I think the town would be lost without it." Indeed, Provincetown misses its late friend.

On Sunday, June 29, 2008, another Blessing of the Fleet was held with Monsignor John Perry conducting the service at MacMillan Pier. A crowd of five hundred attended.

CHAPTER EIGHT

CONTEMPORARY CONCERNS AND TOMORROW'S HISTORY

Only within the moment of time represented by the present century has one species—man—acquired significant power to alter the nature of his world.
—*Rachel Carson, 1907–1964*

It is our task in our time and in our generation, to hand down undiminished to those who come after us, as was handed down to us by those who went before, the natural wealth and beauty which is ours.
—*President John F. Kennedy*

A purist of maritime history may wonder why this last history chapter is contemporary in nature. That's a fair enough question. Cape Cod Bay is a dynamic place with several crucial public policy decisions in motion.

On May 28, 2008, Massachusetts gained the distinction of being the first saltwater state in America with a plan to manage marine development through the Oceans Act of 2008. State Senator Robert O'Leary (D-Cape & Islands) spearheaded the bill, and we have his leadership to thank for this groundbreaking legislation. Governor Deval Patrick signed the bill into law at the New England Aquarium in front of Boston Harbor. "This law will help protect our vital natural resources and balance traditional uses with new ones, such as renewable energy," Patrick insisted. Steve LeBlanc of the Associated Press reported that the "new law requires Massachusetts to make sure all decisions and permits related to state-controlled waters up to three miles from the coast conform to a single, science-based management plan, instead of being considered on a case by case basis."

This mindset comes from the concept of ecosystem-based management, and that fancy term simply means that resource managers and decision makers will take into account what's best for a particular region—from environmental protection to regulating all manner of uses—when deciding on a course of action. The new law calls for an Ocean Advisory Commission composed of a seventeen-member science council, including nine scientists, who will advise Ian Bowles, the secretary of energy and the environment in Massachusetts, on future decisions. "The plan would cover everything from cruise ships and recreational sailing to commercial activities such as liquefied natural gas terminals, wind turbines and the sand and gravel industry."

Environmentalists are hailing the Oceans Act of 2008. Priscilla Brooks of the Conservation Law Foundation said of the legislation, "This will provide a blueprint to enable the state to balance commercial use, personal recreation and the protection of underwater ocean habitats and wildlife."

"We have well-established laws for the use of our land, and now we will have the necessary framework and process in place for the management of one of the Commonwealth's greatest assets—our ocean," Senate President Therese Murray (D-Plymouth) told a gathering at the signing of the bill.

Two industrial energy plants on Cape Cod Bay are vaguely obsolete and are under the watchful eyes of a handful of nonprofit groups. Pine duBois is executive director of the Jones River Watershed Association in Kingston. She works from the Jones River Landing Environmental Heritage Center and is a recent honoree of the Green Star Award by the Environmental League of Massachusetts. DuBois has written about her concerns with the Pilgrim Nuclear Power Plant in Plymouth in the State of the Bay 2007 Report, edited by the author, and issued by the Cape Cod Bay Ocean Sanctuary Program at the Provincetown Center for Coastal Studies:

> During the process of once-through cooling, the plant kills off significant populations of Jones River rainbow smelt and river herring along with impacts to dozens of other fish species. The Pilgrim plant has an intake structure that juts out into the bay to suck in a half billion gallons each day of water to cool the reactor. This water is then discharged back to the bay at high temperatures and questionable quality. The intake structure has screens and mechanisms to prevent too many organisms from being sucked in that would clog the pumps. Nevertheless, hundreds of thousands of fish, larvae and eggs are killed each year as a result of this system.

A second, large industrial site on Cape Cod Bay is the Canal Power Plant. Chris Powicki is president of the Cape & Islands Renewable Energy Collaborative. Writing in the State of the Bay 2007 Report, Powicki noted the "once-through" cooling system emits tons of air pollution into the atmosphere over the bay, along with greenhouse gases and trace amounts of mercury and other air pollutants:

> The Canal Power Plant is the largest steam-electric generating station within Cape Cod Bay's drainage basin. Located on the eastern side of the Cape Cod Canal in Sandwich, it also is a very visible side of our current energy economy, which is large dependent on fossil fuels. Not only is the plant imposing adverse impacts on the bay's water quality, habitats and other species, and coastal communities, but also its mode of operations is indicative of larger problems that could irrevocably alter Cape Cod Bay as we know it.

Clearly energy-related issues could affect the health of Cape Cod Bay in the future. On the horizon of promising changes, under a designation granted by the Environmental Protection Agency, Cape Cod Bay became a No Discharge Area (NDA) on July 14, 2008. This measure, applied for by the Massachusetts Office of Coastal Zone Management, forbids the dumping of treated or untreated sewage anywhere in the bay. The NDA

Working Group, chaired by Steve McKenna of the Massachusetts Office of Coastal Zone Management, gathered data and other information for the application. Dr. Jo Ann Muramoto, senior scientist and Mass. Bays Regional Coordinator for Cape Cod, compiled and composed the application and assisted in helping two towns, Provincetown and Dennis, apply for pumpout facilities. This author—along with Dale Saad of the town of Barnstable; Heather Rockwell, program officer at Nantucket Soundkeeper; Ann Rodney and Regina Lyons of the EPA; and Todd Callaghan of MA CZM—were also in the Cape Cod Bay Working Group. "Nationwide, 25 states have NDAs. All six New England states have part or all of their waters designated as NDAs," explained Muramoto. "In Massachusetts, there are eight NDAs, including six in Cape Cod waters," she added.

The following is from a press released composed by Dr. Muramoto:

> *The waters of Cape Cod Bay deserve more protection because they support regionally important living resources, ecosystems and human uses. Human uses of Cape Cod Bay play an important role in maintaining the Cape's coastal character and economy. Cape Cod Bay provides important shellfishing resources and habitat and is one of the Commonwealth's most important areas for shellfish aquaculture and harvesting. The waters of Cape Cod Bay provide important habitat for fish, wildlife, rare species and marine mammals. Swimming beaches line Cape Cod Bay and attract thousands of tourists annually. Shellfishing, fishing, sightseeing, and boating are just some of the many coastal activities that help to support the Cape's economy.*

Eight NDAs exist in Massachusetts and the Cape Cod Bay NDA would be the largest in the state. Nationwide, twenty-five NDAs are on the books.

Three thousand miles away, in Point Montara, California, aside San Francisco Bay, a lighthouse was discovered to have once stood watch at Mayo Beach in Wellfleet, according to Colleen MacNeney, who told the *Cape Cod Times*, "This is the most exciting thing that I've found." Why the Coast Guard moved the thirty-foot lighthouse out west all the way from Massachusetts is still unsolved; however, the lighthouse remains on duty as an Aid to Navigation. According to reporter Patrick Cassidy, when the lighthouse was operating in Wellfleet Harbor it boasted one of the Lighthouse Service's first female keepers, "Sarah Atwood, who served from 1876 to 1891, following in the job of her late husband, William."

In early June 2008, Yarmouth Conservation Administrator Brad Hall announced the completion of a restoration project to widen a former culvert—now a twelve-foot channel—between two marsh systems within the thirty-five-acre Bass Creek salt marsh, allowing the flow of water to nourish the upper side of the marsh, a formerly drier area. He told the *Cape Cod Times*, "I'm going to guess you are going to see substantial changes in vegetation in the next three to five years." The restoration cost more than $100,000 and was funded primarily through grants written by a wetlands scientist with the Massachusetts Office of Coastal Zone Management, Jeremy Bell.

Ladies' bathing costumes, woven from wool, weighed over ten pounds when wet. *Courtesy of the Historical Society of Old Yarmouth.*

A dragger at work in Yarmouth Port. *Courtesy of the Historical Society of Old Yarmouth.*

Water Quality

Every spring on the water sheet, outings for recreational fishing boats and commercial charters increase. It's also prime sampling season for Dr. Amy Costa of the Provincetown Center for Coastal Studies, who spends many hours aboard the *R/V Alert* at fixed positions near shore and deeper onto the water sheet of Cape Cod Bay.

She says Cape Cod Bay is relatively healthy most of the year, but her data collected over the past several years suggests that anthropogenic, or man-made, influences over the past several years are having a negative impact on the bay. "During the summer months, coincident with the population explosion, water quality conditions begin to deteriorate:

nutrient concentrations increase, dissolved oxygen levels decline, water clarity declines," Costa explained.

Sections along the Cape Cod Bay shoreline show the most wear and tear and evidence of human-based degradation, Costa clarified. "Some of the major threats to coastal waters are pollution, habitat destruction, and overexploitation, all of which result from a combination of commercial, residential, and recreational activities. Cape Cod Bay is susceptible to all of these, and there is evidence of their damage to varying degrees within the bay."

Of course, it's all relative, and doubters may put a spin on current conditions. Compared to Chesapeake Bay, the Gulf of Mexico or Hudson Bay, Costa says Cape Cod Bay may be considered "pristine." But these ecosystems, she adds, for all examined purposes, collapsed before intervention occurred to save them. "Prevention is easier than cure, and to have Cape Cod Bay reach a state of demise without taking preventative measures is unconscionable."

APPENDICES

The following essays represent the perspectives, wisdom and viewpoints of specialists in their fields who have professional interests in, and devotion to, Cape Cod Bay.

Appendix A: Exploring the Cape Cod Bay Shoreline
By Gil Newton, Sandwich High School, Cape Cod Community College

The shoreline of Cape Cod Bay from Marshfield to Provincetown is rich in the diversity of marine plants and animals. Most of these species have washed up on the numerous sandy beaches, but several may live embedded in the hostile intertidal zone, or attached to the many rocks and jetties in front of the beaches. Bring your field guides, a hand lens and a camera to effectively explore these various habitats. You may be surprised at what you will find.

Any exploration starts with the plants, or more accurately in this case, the algae. Commonly called the seaweeds, the marine algae are divided into three main groups based on their pigments: green, brown and red. Depending on the time of the year, you may encounter several different species that vary in shape and size. Green sea lettuce (*Ulva lactuca*) may be found in large sheets, or maybe you will see the notorious and invasive green fleece (*Codium fragile*), which can grow on scallops and other shellfish in large quantities. Attached to rocks and jetties will be the brown rockweed (*Fucus vesiculosus*), determined by its presence of air bladders along the branches. The red algae may be represented by several bright and attractive species, including the edible Irish moss (*Chondrus crispus*) or the pervasive filamentous *Polysiphonia*.

The most common find will be the different seashells along the shore. Many of these species are recognized because of their economic significance. Others are important ecologically, and frequently wash up in enormous numbers. The popular and edible quahaug (*Mercenaria mercenaria*) can be easily identified by its thick shell and purple coloration on the inside. If you see something squirting at you from the substrate, it could be the soft-shell clam (*Mya arenaria*), or steamer. It points its siphon upward for feeding while remaining firmly attached to the substrate with a strong foot. Long, cylindrical razor clams (*Ensis directus*) are often found on mud flats. If you examine the banks on the extensive marshes around the bay, you will find a group of ribbed mussels (*Modiolus demissus*) embedded in the mud.

Another common group of animals are the crustaceans, which includes crabs and shrimp. Usually you can only find a piece of one of these animals, as they are often the victims of larger predators, such as gulls. The perfectly camouflaged spider crab (*Libinia emarginata*) may be concealed by a colony of algae, bryozoans and sponges glued to its shell, or carapace. Be careful if you see a live blue crab (*Callinectes sapidus*). They can pinch, and need to be handled with extreme care. In the salt marsh, you may see the substrate riddled with small holes, which are the homes of the important fiddler crab (*Uca pugnax*). These small animals aerate and fertilize the marsh, and are a major food source for other animals. By the way, the male is the one with the large claw.

Of course, one animal that may be seen is commonly mistaken as a crab, and that is the horseshoe crab (*Limulus polyphemus*). This animal is more closely related to arachnids, such as spiders and ticks. It evolved millions of years ago, and today is known for its contributions to medical science. Harmless to you, it feeds mainly on worms and clams.

Appendix B: Cape Cod National Seashore
By William Burke, Historian and Cultural Resources Program Manager,
Cape Cod National Seashore

On August 7, 1961, when President John F. Kennedy signed the legislation establishing Cape Cod National Seashore, he declared, "I…hope that this will be one of a whole series of great seashore parks which will be for the inspiration and enjoyment of people all over the United States." Since then, other national seashores indeed have been created, but Cape Cod's has become one of the nation's most popular parks, with more than five million visitors each year. Most recognize the multiple benefits the seashore provides, including the realization of former Senator Leverett Saltonstall's dream of maintaining Cape Cod "so that other Americans, in dire need of the natural grandeur of the clean, open spaces, will find an outlet from their crowded, grimy, urban lives." Upon passage of the bill creating the seashore, the *Berkshire Eagle* of Pittsfield editorialized, "The bill can probably be labeled the finest victory ever recorded for the cause of conservation in New England."

The National Seashore's forty-four thousand acres, consisting of both land and offshore waters, includes miles of pristine shoreline on Cape Cod Bay. Seashore planners became aware of not only the bay's warm waters and gentle drop, which offered safe swimming for families, but also that the bay represented a treasure-trove of local history. The bay's protected harbors, coves and islands offered sanctuary for early peoples living here. Native Indians settled along the bay for thousands of years. The discovery of an ossuary (the technical term for a multiple burial) on Wellfleet's Indian Neck in the late 1970s points to an advanced society. European explorers like Gosnold and Champlain noted the bay's extreme abundance of fish and whales. The Pilgrims aboard the *Mayflower* in 1620 circumnavigated the bay before choosing Plymouth as their permanent home, but crossed back over the bay decades later to farm and fish. Shore whaling continued into the 1700s, and Smith Tavern, situated on the bluffs above the bay on Great Island, provided hospitality to local boat crews. At Provincetown's superb deep-water harbor, settlers took advantage of the bay's natural bounty and established a whaling and fishing port unequaled in the region. Settlements that nestled along the shores of the bay at Long Point, Race Point and Bound Brook eventually declined as some of the bay's resources waned and inlets closed due to sand accretion.

Today, the seashore's Bay shoreline represents a different sort of sanctuary: a place to escape the swirl of summer's rush. It doesn't have the biggest waves or the famous beaches of the Outer Cape's back side. Here, though, you have an honest chance to leave the world behind—just you and the glistening pebbles on the beach at Duck Harbor. Or walk with a companion out across Hatches Harbor Dike to rediscover the sweep of Race Point Lighthouse. The longest and most challenging official seashore trail, the Great Island Trail (eight miles round trip), runs past the old tavern site until the trail vanishes in the surf at Jeremy Point. In short, at the seashore, where land meets bay, there is a chance that the only footprints you'll encounter will be your own on your return trip from wherever. Truly, the shores of Cape Cod Bay continue to be a sanctuary for all to enjoy at Cape Cod National Seashore.

Appendix C: Areas of Critical Environmental Concern Program, Massachusetts Department of Conservation and Recreation
By Lisa G. Berry-Engler, Coastal Coordinator

For more information, please visit the ACEC website at http://www.mass.gov/dcr/stewardship/acec. Areas of Critical Environmental Concern (ACECs) are places in Massachusetts that receive special recognition because of the quality, uniqueness and significance of their natural and cultural resources. These areas are identified and nominated at the community level and are reviewed and designated by the state's secretary of energy and environmental affairs (formerly the secretary of environmental affairs). The purpose of the ACEC Program is to preserve, restore and enhance critical environmental resources and resource areas of the Commonwealth of Massachusetts. Identification and designation of these ecological areas, increasing the level of protection for ACECs and facilitating and supporting the stewardship of ACECs are the goals of the ACEC Program. ACEC designation increases public awareness and provides education about the exceptional ecological and cultural resources within the ACEC. ACEC designation also creates a framework for local and regional stewardship of critical resources and ecosystems.

Established in 1975 by legislation that instituted the Massachusetts Executive Office of Environmental Affairs, the ACEC Program has worked to protect the state's critical resources for more than thirty years. Currently, the ACEC Program oversees the preservation, restoration and enhancement of a wealth of diverse cultural and natural resources in twenty-eight coastal and inland ACECs. Fourteen of these ACECs are considered coastal, in that they lie within the coastal zone (the area between three miles offshore and one hundred feet beyond the first major land transportation route encountered on shore (a road, highway, rail line, etc.) and including all of Cape Cod and the Islands). Of the fourteen coastal ACECs, nine are found in the Cape Cod/ Plymouth region and four border Cape Cod Bay. The Ellisville Harbor ACEC is located in the town of Plymouth and was designated in 1980. The Inner Cape Cod Bay ACEC, designated in 1985, is found within the towns of Brewster, Eastham and Orleans. The oldest of the Cape Cod ACECs, the Sandy Neck Barrier Beach System ACEC, was designated in 1978 and is located within Barnstable and Sandwich. Lastly, the largest of the Cape Cod Bay ACECs, Wellfleet Harbor ACEC, is found in the outer Cape towns of Eastham and Truro and was designated more recently in 1989.

These Cape Cod Bay ACECs total approximately 24,805 acres and include salt marshes, estuaries, barrier beaches, coastal dunes, tidal flats, coastal flood plains, salt ponds and tidal creeks and rivers. The critical natural resources within these ACECs provide feeding and breeding grounds for many aquatic birds, habitats for shellfish and finfish, improved water quality and recreational opportunities for the public, as well as storm damage protection and flood storage capacity for neighboring communities. Sixteen state-listed threatened or endangered species and two federally listed threatened or endangered species find refuge within these ACECs. Archaeological sites abound at the margins of these coastal resource areas where prehistoric and historic populations lived, scavenged and fished. The Sandy Neck ACEC includes a wealth of archaeologically significant sites, so much so that the entire area is designated a significant historical site by the Massachusetts Historical Commission. But the Wellfleet Harbor ACEC contains the most archaeological sites of the Cape Cod Bay ACECs, at seventy-five. These sites include historic shell middens, individual burial sites and a mass grave discovered in the late 1970s.

Stewardship plays a key role in the protection of ACEC resources post-designation. ACEC stewards can be local, state or federal organizations, individuals or a collaborative partnership amongst all or some of these groups. The ACEC Program relies heavily on stewards of ACEC resources to guide stewardship activities, set priorities for individual ACECs and help develop a comprehensive understanding of the threats and demands of the community. Stewards possess a strong interest in the protection of the ACEC resources and help raise awareness for the critical ACEC resources, their value to the community and how to provide protection from threats such as development, water-quality degradation, overuse and mismanagement. The Cape Cod Bay ACEC stewardship groups' activities include drafting management documents such as barrier beach management plans or harbor management plans, educating users through signage, pamphlets or guided walks, supporting scientific research and holding annual conferences. The Cape Cod Bay ACECs' stewardship groups vary in their goals and activity levels, but each provides a tailored approach to the protection of the ACEC resources.

Appendix D: Commercial Finfisheries in Cape Cod Bay
By Jeremy King, Fisheries Biologist, Massachusetts Division of Marine Fisheries

Cape Cod Bay finfisheries have changed over the last few decades. Regulatory measures enacted to rebuild regional groundfish populations (Atlantic cod, yellowtail flounder, winter flounder, etc.) have restrained fishing operations using gear capable of catching groundfish. In addition, directed fisheries for spiny dogfish have also been limited by strict catch quotas and closed seasons. These measures have reduced otter trawl and gillnet fisheries in Cape Cod Bay. As these vessels have become less active in Cape Cod Bay finfisheries, a large fleet of small boat fishermen who pursue species such as striped bass, bluefish, bluefin tuna and summer flounder with hook and line have become the more active fleet. These fishermen work out of all ports surrounding Cape Cod Bay and are difficult to distinguish from recreational fishermen. Over three hundred hook and line fishermen reported selling striped bass caught in Cape Cod Bay in 2006.

A fleet of approximately three dozen otter trawl vessels continues to fish Cape Cod Bay on a limited basis. Otter trawl vessels (typically forty-five to sixty-five feet) that fish Cape Cod Bay tie up in Provincetown, Sandwich and Plymouth Harbors, as well as numerous more distant Massachusetts ports. These trawlers typically fish with large mesh nets designed to retain only legal-size groundfish. However, an otter trawl fishery for whiting pursued in a defined area, including outer Cape Cod Bay, features a modified small mesh otter trawl designed to minimize groundfish bycatch by having less bottom contact. Whiting have not been abundant in the defined area at the time (fall) this fishery is allowed over the last couple of years, resulting in less participation in this once active fishery.

A small fleet of approximately ten vessels deploys gillnets in Cape Cod Bay on a limited basis. These fishermen reported bluefish, dogfish, skates and monkfish as their largest catches in 2006, followed by Atlantic cod. Fish pot fisheries, which are more active in warmer waters south and west of Cape Cod, pursue black sea bass, tautog and scup on a smaller scale in Cape Cod Bay. Five vessels reported setting fish pots in Cape Cod Bay during 2006.

A purse seine fishery targeting giant bluefin tuna occurs in Cape Cod Bay when bluefin tuna schools migrate in. The effort by these vessels (number of sets) is typically very small and occurs on only a few days of any given year in Cape Cod Bay, but the catches can be large when the tuna are in. No tuna seine sets were made in 2006.

Recreational Finfisheries

Recreational fishing opportunities are abundant in Cape Cod Bay. Recreational anglers pursue a variety of species including striped bass, fluke, winter flounder, mackerel, bluefin tuna, bluefish and Atlantic cod. Shore anglers fish the surf and harbors, while a ubiquitous fleet of private boats and an extensive fleet of party boats carry a host of anglers to all reaches of Cape Cod Bay.

Fishery Survey Trends

The Massachusetts Division of Marine Fisheries has conducted a trawl survey every spring and fall since 1978 throughout state waters, including Cape Cod Bay. The survey is useful in monitoring population trends in many fish species that reside on or near the seafloor of Cape Cod Bay, including species of little commercial or recreational interest. As is true in the greater Gulf of Maine, many of the commercially important groundfish species (American plaice, Atlantic cod, winter flounder and yellowtail flounder) have declined in Cape Cod Bay over the survey time series. Ocean pout, not part of the regulatory "groundfish species" group, has experienced one of the greatest declines in the survey, while little skate, spiny dogfish and longhorn sculpin have generally increased in the spring survey. Winter skate biomass has remained low since 1990, but is showing slow increase. Red hake biomass has dropped after highs in the late 1990s.

Appendix E: Right Whales Through the Lens of History
By Charles "Stormy" Mayo, Senior Scientist, Provincetown Center for Coastal Studies

It's virtually impossible to know with any accuracy how important Cape Cod Bay is to right whales, because we really don't understand the specific balances between food and the energetic requirements of the animals, much less how many habitats are available when Cape Cod Bay is at its peak. So it's possible that there are many other places that would substitute quite nicely for Cape Cod Bay to support the whales in their foraging activities. That said, the long history and high regularity of the bay in supporting right whales during the midwinter and early spring is highly suggestive of a habitat that has been and continues to be important to the animals, at least in, if you will, their perspective. We do know that the resource, the zooplankton, in Cape Cod Bay is particularly rich. If one were to take a long view of the question, I think it would be possible to say that Cape Cod Bay contributes an important resource to the right whales, one that in some way or another would compromise them if it were removed from their view.

It is very hard to know, even after nearly twenty-five years of looking, exactly what parameters make the bay so important to the formation of the patches that the right whales require. It certainly is possible to say that whatever those conditions are, they result in an unbelievably rich if ephemeral concentration of zooplankton. There are some suggestions within our data that a combination of low flushing rates, particularly in the eastern part of the bay, with the location of Cape Cod at the southern terminus of the Gulf of Maine and the inclusion of a persistent southward moving current, combine to bring the plankton resources into the area.

The 2008 season was as best I can tell unique among the twenty-five years of our study. Although whales came in and departed at approximately the same time, the number residing in the bay appears to have been between two and three times greater than the previous greatest number. We don't know exactly how many whales were present in Cape Cod Bay this year (that depends upon the aerial survey team's analysis), but it seems likely that as many as two hundred animals, and perhaps more, were present in the bay at some point during the 2008 season. Not unexpectedly, that resource that supported the animals and the amount of their feeding was greater than we've observed in past years.

I think the population of the right whale of the North Atlantic will likely teeter in the low hundreds for a considerable amount of time. The teetering will go positive when the Atlantic biology and the willingness of people ringing the Atlantic to control certain kinds of fishing and shipping activities conspire to make a more comfortable ocean basin for right whales and other species. In the case of the right whale, we clearly must control the increasing death from ship and fishing activity, as you know, and so it is unlikely that right whales will be able to recover from this very low population number if mortality, which has been increasing, continues to do so. It's not hard to see that if the population was dropped to extremely low numbers, as we know it was in the late nineteenth century, and if the whales cannot recover apparently because of ship strikes and entanglement, that the stasis in which they find themselves will likely begin to go negative irreversibly if the causes of mortality increase. That said, I think in the near term, over the next century, with increasing sensitivity to the causes of mortality, the right whales will likely very slowly increase in numbers in the North Atlantic.

NOTES ON CONTENT,
RESEARCH AND
COMPOSITION PROCESSES

Chapter One: Where Geology Meets
Early Scientific Research

Examining the geologic context of Cape Cod Bay inspired Chapter One. To me, it was a necessity and valid prelude to proceeding chapters. How can we examine the cultural dynamics of this ecosystem over several hundred years without understanding how Cape Cod Bay was "made"? I turned to two scientists for data and answers and explanations that even an English major could understand; the collective research of Robert Oldale and Graham Giese, whose research over decades has led to solid review and understanding of the natural processes within Cape Cod Bay, and they proved invaluable.

Chapter Two: People of the First Light

Native American history in New England has been extensively researched. Original documents are accessible at museums, research facilities and within secondary sources, including tomes authored by Howard S. Russell and the Editor, Simeon Deyo. A crucial juncture in native culture was King Philip's War, and I relied on *King Philip's War* by Michael J. Tougias and Eric B. Schultz. Hartman Deetz, a former interpreter in the Wampanoag settlement at Plimoth Plantation, shared research about daily and seasonal family life of native people, a subject unendingly fascinating to me.

Chapter Three: Europeans Wash Ashore

This was a challenging chapter to compose, for it involved knitting facts of many explorers' travels in, around and near Cape Cod Bay over a concentrated timeline, and containing those data only as they related to the history of Cape Cod Bay. Not always an easy task, since I tend to digress when I'm genuinely interested in a topic. Navigating what should be included was challenging but well worth the time investment. I am not a fan of deciphering sixteenth- and seventeenth-century English, and it's not a timeline I'm wholly familiar with, unlike, say, the nineteenth century.

Chapter Four: Permanence on Cape Cod Bay

As a writer of topics of the past, I sometimes wonder where early American history would be without William Bradford's poignant recollection of those early hours, days, weeks and months following the *Mayflower*'s arrival in Provincetown Harbor and, latterly, Cape Cod Bay. Eleanor Hammond of the Bourne Historical Society shared her twenty years of research of the Aptucxet Trading Post. Finding original research is challenging because, in relative terms to the nineteenth century, much isn't there from the 1600s, save the oft-repeated stories, biographies and autobiographical accounts of seventeenth-century yesteryear. One new element about Cape Cod Bay that I had not known before starting this project, and loved researching, was the onetime opening between Nauset and Cape Cod Bay, which essentially made the Lower Cape its own island for a short time. David Kew's website on Cape Cod history and Captain Cyprian Southack's account of using that shallow waterway added newer pieces of data added to the dialogue. Duncan Oliver and the late Jack Braginton-Smith's book on shore whaling deserved more time and space than I could give it, but proved one of the most valuable secondary sources in use in this book.

Chapter Five: Boiling Points

Years ago I composed an essay about the infamous Boston Tea Party for *The Cape Cod Voice* and used it in my first book for The History Press, *True Accounts of Yankee Ingenuity and Grit*. Rather than reinvent the wheel, I changed a few things and boldly repeated it to kick off Chapter Five. Few aficionados of the American Revolution link Cape Cod to its larger geographic familiar presence of Boston proper, so I felt the piece was worth recycling. The tragedy of the *General Arnold* came from the account by Barnabas Downs, who survived the 1778 ice storm that lodged the vessel in ice off Plymouth. John Grenier extensively studied John Gorham of Barnstable, who fought in northern wars off Cape Cod, but I included Gorham since his story was emblematic of native Cape Codders who left and engaged in warfare elsewhere. Gorham's story is not directly related to Cape Cod Bay, but it shows how the resource was used as a maritime highway over which he no doubt sailed. The making of salt from sun and sea marked the launch of a new industry that originated on Cape Cod Bay and helped sustain residents along its shores. I relied on Nancy Thacher Reid's book, *Dennis, Cape Cod*. Additionally, four essays in this chapter that I composed for *The Cape Cod Voice* best reflect the tensions and uniqueness of British-American relations in the eighteenth and nineteenth centuries. Writing about the Battle of Orleans was extremely frustrating; certainly the most detailed account of facts that required meticulous care, because the story shifted frequently, and often with simultaneous actions between the American and British. Needless to say, I was very happy when that chapter was finished.

Chapter Six: Industry and Family

The story of fish stocks in American waters and the natural richness we pull from the marine environment deserves more than a chapter. Clearly the finfish, shellfish, bivalves and other food harvested from Cape Cod Bay no doubt meant the difference between starvation and life to early colonists. The story of how wood and water evolved into thriving business and related industries in American waters deserves more than a chapter. But I attempted to capture the spirit of these two areas of research only as they apply to the maritime history of Cape Cod Bay. I felt exploring family life would complement another area of research since history, after all, is about real people: who they were, what they did and how they behaved.

Chapter Seven: Progress and a New Century

When I told my friend Susan Davenport about this book, she showed me a photograph of the *Alice May Davenport* that hangs in her back hall. It seemed a perfect and appropriate subject to begin this chapter early in the nineteenth century, when the vessel was encased in ice off North Dennis for a wicked long time in the winter of 1905. Nothing says progress more on Cape Cod Bay than a huge canal and bridges to match. Some of the information about the canal came from Samantha Mirabella, a park ranger for the U.S. Army Corps of Engineers who contributed to the first-ever State State of the Bay Report, which I edited in 2007. Noel Beyle's book on the infamous target ship, the SS *James Longstreet*, was very helpful. Fisheries biologist Jeremy King's enthusiasm for the nuances of Cape Cod Bay contributed to the body of knowledge about why the Provincetown-area fishery was successful. I remember a conversation with the late Louie Rivers of Provincetown about the annual Blessing of the Fleet there, and how a land-based annual event commemorated the age-old and time-honored practice of fishing. Clearly Provincetown deserves not only its own chapter, but its own book.

Chapter Eight: Contemporary Concerns and Tomorrow's History

As I wrapped this book project, bay-related events appeared in the news. Between the passage of the Oceans Act of 2008 and the designation of Cape Cod Bay as a No Discharge Area by the Environmental Protection Agency on July 14 at Sesuit Harbor in East Dennis, we're seeing history in the making, so I dedicated the last chapter to contemporary issues. What's happening on Cape Cod Bay today will affect the health of the ecosystem in the future, and if done so negatively, will have an impact on our ability to safeguard and preserve Cape Cod Bay's cultural heritage. I don't regret steering readers toward the present in chapter eight, but I imagine historians won't approve of this digression. Onward. I found that resource managers, decision makers and even those in the subfields of historical preservation are passionate about Cape Cod Bay and have dedicated many professional hours to its study and health. But I am saddened to think that the words in those ancient journals and diaries from pioneers like William Bradford, Captain John Smith and others often fail to fully capture the respect they had for Cape Cod Bay. If they were before us today, what would they say?

BIBLIOGRAPHY

Books

Adams, Henry. *The War of 1812.* New York: First Cooper Press, 1999.

Bangs, Jeremy Dupertuis. *Indian Deeds: Land Transactions in Plymouth County, 1620–1691.* Boston: New England Historic Genealogical Society, 2002.

Barbo, Theresa Mitchell. *True Accounts of Yankee Ingenuity and Grit from The Cape Cod Voice.* Charleston, SC: The History Press, 2007.

Barnard, Ruth L. *A History of Early Orleans.* Orleans, MA: Orleans Historical Society, 1975.

Bartlett, Irving H. *Wendell Phillips-Brahmin Radical.* Toronto: S.J. Reginald Saunders and Company, 1961.

Beyle, Noel W. *The Target Ship in Cape Cod Bay.* Falmouth, MA: Kendall Printing, 1978.

Bourne, Russell. *The View From Front Street: Travels Through New England's Historic Fishing Communities.* Markham, Ontario: Penguin Books Canada, Ltd., 1989.

Bradford, William. *Of Plymouth Plantation, 1620–1647.* New York: The Modern Library, 1856.

Broadhurst, Francis I. *A History of the U.S. Custom House and Post Office Building.* Barnstable: Coast Guard Heritage Museum.

Bunting, W.H. *Portrait of a Port.* Cambridge, MA: First Harvard University Press, 1971.

Cahill, Robert Ellis. *New England's Viking and Indian Wars.* New England's Collectible Classics. [Further information unavailable.]

Cape Cod Library of Local History and Genealogy. Compiled and indexed by Leonard H. Smith Jr. Baltimore, MD: Genealogical Publishing Co., Inc., 1992.

Carpenter, Delores Bird. *Early Encounters—Native Americans and Europeans in New England*. East Lansing: Michigan State University Press. 1994.

Colonial Society in Massachusetts. *Seafaring in Colonial Massachusetts*. Boston: The Colonial Society of Massachusetts, 1975.

Conway, J. North. *The Cape Cod Canal: Breaking Through the Bared and Bended Arm*. Charleston, SC: The History Press, 2008.

Coogan, Jim, and Jack Sheedy. *Cape Cod Companion—The History and Mystery of Old Cape Cod*. East Dennis, MA: Harvest Home Books. 1999.

Darling, Warren S. *Quahoging Out of Rock Harbor, 1890–1930*. Orleans, MA: Warren S. Darling at Thompson's Printing, Inc., 1984.

Deetz, James, and Patricia Scott Deetz. *The Times of Their Lives: Life, Love, and Death in Plymouth Colony*. New York: W.H. Freeman and Company, 2000.

Downs, Barnabas. *Shipwreck in Plymouth Harbour*. Yarmouth Port, MA: Parnassus Imprints. 1972.

Freeman, Frederick. *The History of Cape Cod: The Annals of Barnstable County*. Boston: Printed for the author, 1858.

Freeman, James. *A Description of the Eastern Coast of the County of Barnstable*. Boston: Hosea Sprague, No. 44 Marlboro' Street, 1802.

Gookin, Daniel. *Historical Collections of the Indians in New England*. Boston: Belknap and Hall, 1674.

Gookin, Warner F. *Bartholomew Gosnold: Discoverer and Planter*. Hamden, CT: Archon Books, 1963.

Grenier, John. *The First Way of War: American War Making on the Frontier*. New York: Cambridge University Press, 2005.

History of Barnstable County, Massachusetts. Edited by Simeon L. Deyo. New York: H.W. Blake & Co., 1890.

James, Sydney V., Jr. *Three Visitors to Early Plymouth*. Bedford, MA, 1963.

Johnston, James C., Jr. *The Yankee Fleet: Maritime New England in the Age of Sail*. Charleston, SC: The History Press, 2007.

King, H. Roger. *Cape Cod and Plymouth Colony in the Seventeenth Century*. Lanham, MD: University Press of America, 1994.

Kittredge, Henry C. *Cape Cod, Its People and Their History*. Boston: Houghton Mifflin, 1963.

———. *Shipmasters of Cape Cod*. Hyannis, MA: Parnassus Imprints, 1998.

Linholdt, Paul J. *John Josselyn, Colonial Traveler—A Critical Edition of Two Voyages to New England*. Hanover, NH: University Press of New England, 1988.

Mahoney, Haynes. *Yarmouth's Proud Packets*. Yarmouth Port, MA: The Historical Society of Old Yarmouth, 1986.

Miller, Stauffer. *Hoisting Their Colors: Cape Cod's Civil War Navy Officers*. Charlottesville, VA: XLibris Corporation, 2008.

Morison, Samuel Eliot. *Maritime History of Massachusetts, 1783–1860*. Cambridge, MA: Riverside Press, 1921.

Otis, Amos. *Genealogical Notes of Barnstable Families*. Barnstable, MA: F.B. & F.P. Goss, 1888.

Paine, Joan. *Cape Cod Masters of the Seas*. Brewster, MA: Wrackline Writers, 2000.

Philbrick, Nathaniel. *Mayflower: A Story of Courage, Community, and War*. New York: Viking, 2006.

Prince, Thomas. *The New England Chronicles*. Boston: Thomas Prince, Jr., 1736.

Quinn, David B., and Alison M. Quinn, eds. *The English New England Voyages, 1602–1608*. Cambridge, England: University Press, 1980.

Quinn, William P. *Cape Cod Maritime Disasters*. Orleans, MA: Lower Cape Publishing, 1990.

Reid, Nancy Thacher. *Dennis, Cape Cod, From Firstcomers to Newcomers, 1639–1993*. Dennis, MA: Dennis Historical Society, 1996.

Rich, Shebnah. *Truro Cape Cod*. Boston: D. Lothrop and Company, 1883.

Russell, Howard S. *Indian New England Before the Mayflower.* Hanover, NH: University Press of New England, 1980.

Schultz, Eric B., and Michael J. Tougias. *King Philip's War, The History and Legacy of America's Forgotten Conflict.* Woodstock, VT: The Countryman Press, 1999.

Schwarzman, Beth. *The Nature of Cape Cod.* Hanover, NH: University Press of New England, 2002.

Smith, John, Captain. *A Description of New England; Observations and Discoveries in the North of America In The Year of Our Lord, 1614.* Boston: William Veazie, 1865.

Smith, Leonard H., Jr. *Cape Cod Library of Local History and Genealogy.* Baltimore, MD: Genealogical Publishing Co., 1922.

Thoreau, Henry David. *Cape Cod.* Chatham, MA: The Peninsula Press, 1997.

Tuchman, Barbara W. *The First Salute, A View of the American Revolution.* New York: Alfred A. Knopf, 1988.

Whalen, Richard F. *Everyday Life in Truro, From the Indians to the Victorians.* Charleston, SC: The History Press, 2007.

———. *Truro: the Story of a Cape Cod Town.* Charleston, SC: The History Press, 2007.

Winslow, Edward. *Mourt's Relation, A Journal of the Pilgrims at Plymouth.* Bedford, MA: Applewood Books, 1622.

Manuscripts, Documents and Other Sources

Account Book of Francis Jackson, Treasurer, the Vigilance Committee of Boston
American Lighthouse Foundation
American Philosophical Society
Associated Press
Barnstable Historical Commission
Bourne Historical Society
Cape & Islands Renewable Energy Collaborative
Cape Cod Commission
Dennis Historical Society
Environmental Protection Agency
Hallett, Leaman F. "Indian Trails and Their Importance to the Early Colonists."
Historic Cultural Land Use Study of Lower Cape Cod: A Study of the Historical Archaeology and History of the Cape Cod National Seashore and the Surrounding Region

Historical Society of Old Yarmouth

Jones River Watershed Association

Lawson, Ellen McKenzie, PhD. "The Roaring Twenties on the Cape and Islands: A History of Rumrunning and Prohibition, 1920–33."

National Archives

National Oceanic and Atmospheric Administration

National Parks Service

Old Sturbridge Village

Plimoth Plantation

State of the Bay 2007, edited by Theresa M. Barbo, Provincetown Center for Coastal Studies

U.S. Army Corps of Engineers

U.S. Coast Guard

Woods Hole Oceanographic Institution

Periodicals and Articles

The American Neptune Journal of Maritime History

Barnstable Patriot

Boston Herald

The Cape Cod Times

Rose, Mark. "Origins of Syphilis." *Archaeology Magazine* 50, no. 1 (January/February 1997).

United States Coast Pilot, Atlantic Coast, Department of Commerce

Yarmouth Register

INDEX

ABOUT THE AUTHOR

Theresa Mitchell Barbo has researched, written and lectured on Cape Cod maritime and cultural history for nearly twenty years. She is a former broadcast journalist and history editor at *The Cape Cod Voice*. She is a member of the Cape Cod Bay No Discharge Area Working Group, which successfully petitioned the Environmental Protection Agency to prohibit the dumping of treated or raw sewage into the bay. Theresa is also the editor of the first ever State of the Bay 2007 Report. She holds BA and MA degrees from the University of Massachusetts Dartmouth and completed the Executive Integral Leadership Program at the Mendoza College of Business at the University of Notre Dame.

Theresa resides in Yarmouth Port, not far from Cape Cod Bay, with her husband, Daniel, and their children, Katherine Margaret and Thomas.

Also by Theresa Mitchell Barbo:

The Cape Cod Murder of 1899: Edwin Ray Snow's Punishment and Redemption
The Pendleton Disaster off Cape Cod: The Greatest Small Boat Rescue in Coast Guard History
True Accounts of Yankee Ingenuity and Grit from The Cape Cod Voice

Visit us at
www.historypress.net